MONTGOMERY

MILITARY PROFILES

SERIES EDITOR
Dennis E. Showalter, Ph.D.
Colorado College

Instructive summaries for general and expert readers alike, volumes in the Military Profiles series are essential treatments of significant and popular military figures drawn from world history, ancient times through the present.

MONTGOMERY

D-Day Commander

Nigel Hamilton

Potomac Books, Inc.
Washington, D.C.

Library of Congress Cataloging-in-Publication Data
Hamilton, Nigel.
   Montgomery : D-Day commander / Nigel Hamilton. — 1st ed.
      p. cm. — (Military profiles)
   Includes bibliographical references and index.
   ISBN 1-57488-903-6 (hardcover : alk. paper) — ISBN 1-57488-904-4 (pbk. : alk. paper)
   1. Montgomery of Alamein, Bernard Law Montgomery, Viscount, 1887–1976. 2. Marshals—Great Britain—Biography. 3. Great Britain. Army—Biography. I. Title.
   DA69.3.M56H344 2006
   940.54'21092—dc22
   [B]
                                        2006018360

ISBN-10 1-57488-903-6 HC
ISBN-13 978-1-57488-903-1 HC
ISBN-10 1-57488-904-4 PB
ISBN-13 978-1-57488-904-8 PB

Printed in the United States of America on acid-free paper that meets the American National Standards Institute Z39-48 Standard.

Potomac Books, Inc.
22841 Quicksilver Drive
Dulles, Virginia 20166

First Edition

10 9 8 7 6 5 4 3 2 1

Contents

Maps

Preface

Field-Marshal Bernard Law Montgomery has had poor posthumous press coverage in America. Even in his home country, Britain, Montgomery remains a controversial figure: undoubtedly one of the great captains of the twentieth century, and yet so arrogant, so insubordinate, and so boastful that most historians never warm to him as a historical personality.

Like Gen. George S. Patton, Montgomery—"Monty"—always felt he knew best. Or, as he put it more precisely, he knew best "*how to beat the Germans.*" Given the early performance of the Allied European armies in World War II in Norway and at Dunkirk, and of the American forces initially in North Africa in 1942, this was no exaggeration. Somehow, in the space of a few months, these two commanders, Montgomery and Patton, transformed their armies until they were able to compete against a well-armed, well-trained, and well-commanded enemy. Both Patton and Montgomery, who landed side by side in southern Sicily in the summer of 1943, learned "the invasion ropes": how to train their men to assault an enemy in a contested amphibious landing, how get their troops ashore—and how, once established there, to use a punch to the solar plexus, followed by a left or right hook, to finish off the opponent. This was a critical education, and it laid the foundation of the greatest of all Allied battles of World War II, namely, the invasion of Normandy in 1944—D-Day.

That General Patton, as an American, came to feel so much rivalry for his British co-commander and Allied comrade-in-arms should not surprise us—for both men were profoundly competitive, prima donnas who were perhaps bound to collide. Had they been blessed with better generals above them, they would, I believe, be seen more clearly today as the greatest *pair* of battlefield commanders of all history. Montgomery's iron grip and charismatic command of his British troops and Patton's grasp of modern American armored tactical warfare made them a formidable combination. Indeed, against them even the finest German commanders, including Rommel, Kesselring, and Runstedt, had no chance.

Allied generals Dwight D. Eisenhower and Sir Harold Alexander, by contrast, were nice men but ineffective battlefield directors. As commander in chief and deputy commander in chief in the Mediterranean Theater of the war, Eisenhower and Alexander's direction of the Allied landings and campaign in Sicily was abysmal, resulting in the successful evacuation from Sicily of almost the entire defending German army in late August 1943, and in an even more miserable Allied performance on the mainland of Italy thereafter.

Patton and Montgomery, however, learned many vital lessons from the Sicilian campaign—lessons that were to prove crucial a year later, on the coast of France. The D-Day invasion and the Battle of Normandy which followed it were the greatest examples of strategic, tactical, armored, and inter-Allied warfare in modern history—backed by air and naval forces. Had the D-Day landings failed, or the Allied bridgehead in France been overwhelmed by Rommel's forces, the course and even the outcome of World War II would have been completely different.

Why D-Day succeeded is the theme of this small book. It is a study of one kind of leadership, exemplified by one man's actions in combat. There were, of course, many types of leadership displayed in World War II, as well as great self-sacrificing courage and endurance on the part of millions of men and women. But in the end, as even supreme commander General Eisenhower privately acknowledged, D-Day was Montgomery's triumph. "I don't know if we could have done it without Monty," Eisenhower later confided. "It was his sort of battle. Whatever they say about him, he got us there."[1]

Understanding how Monty "got" the Allies there; how he made D-Day his "sort" of battle; and how he commanded the four Allied land armies in the great three-month battle of Normandy—leading to the triumphant Allied crossing of the Seine at the end of August 1944—as well as two American armies in the Battle of the Bulge, will, I hope, help us to appreciate his enduring, if controversial, place in military history.

Chronology

November 17, 1887	Born in Kennington, South London.
January 1902	After childhood spent in Tasmania, Australia, enters army class at St. Paul's School, London.
January 30, 1907	Cadet, Royal Military College, Sandhurst.
December 12, 1908	Joins 1st Battalion, Royal Warwickshire Regiment, on NW frontier of India, as 2nd lieutenant.
November 6, 1912	1st Battalion, Royal Warwickshire Regiment, returns to England.

World War I

August 21, 1914	1st Battalion, Royal Warwickshire Regiment, leaves England to join British Expeditionary Force in Belgium (retreat from Mons).
October 13, 1914	Battle of Meteren—severely wounded in chest, grave dug—survives—awarded Distinguished Service Order—promoted to captain.
February 12, 1915 *through* *November 11, 1918*	Brigade-Major, 112 Infantry Brigade, England—posted to western front—takes part in Battle of Somme (1916), Arras (1917), Pass-chendaele (1917), Lys (1918), Chemin-des-Dames (1918), then as lieutenant-colonel and chief of staff, 47th Division, Battle of Amiens (1918).

Interwar Years

March 24, 1919	Staff major, British Occupation Army, Cologne.
September 5, 1919	Commanding officer, 17th Battalion, Royal Fusiliers, Ruhr.

January 20, 1920	Student, Staff College, Camberley.
December 18, 1920	Brigade-major, Cork Infantry Brigade, Ireland, during the "Troubles."
1923–25	Training officer, 49th Territorial Division, York (volunteer reserve soldiers).
July 28, 1925	Instructor, Staff College, Camberley.
July 27, 1927	Marries Mrs. Betty Carver, née Hobart, London.
Summer 1929	Appointed to write new edition of War Office Infantry Training Manual, Woking.
January 1930	Promoted to substantive rank of lieutenant-colonel. As commanding officer, 1st Battalion, Royal Warwickshire Regiment embarks for Middle East, where he also becomes officer commanding all British troops in Palestine.
December 1932	1st Battalion posted to Alexandria, Egypt, part of Canal Brigade.
December 24, 1933	1st Battalion posted to Poona, India.
June 29, 1934	Promoted to full colonel and chief instructor, Staff College, Quetta, NW Frontier, India.
August 5, 1937	Promoted to brigadier, commanding 9th Infantry Brigade, Portsmouth.
October 19, 1937	Mrs. Betty Montgomery dies.
October 11, 1938	Promoted to major-general, commanding 8th Division, Palestine.
May 24, 1939	Mystery illness, thought to be tuberculosis— evacuated to England.
August 26, 1939	Unemployed.
August 28, 1939	Major-general commanding 3rd (Iron) Division, Portsmouth.

World War II

September 29, 1939	3rd Division posted to France as part of new British Expeditionary Force.
May 29, 1940	3rd Division retreats to La Panne, near Dunkirk.
May 30, 1940	Appointed corps commander, 2nd Corps, La Panne.

June 1, 1940	Evacuated from Dunkirk to England.
November 17, 1941	Lieutenant-general, commander, South-Eastern Army, United Kingdom.
August 8, 1942	Appointed to command 8th Army at Alamein, Egypt.
August 31–September 7, 1942	Battle of Alam Halfa—Rommel withdraws.
October 24–November 4, 1942	Battle of Alamein—Rommel retreats across North Africa to Tunisia.
November 11, 1942	Promoted to full general.
July 10, 1943	Allied invasion of Sicily—8th Army lands alongside 7th U.S. Army.
August 1943	Battle of Sicily ends with fall of Messina.
September 3, 1943	8th Army invasion of mainland of Italy at Reggio.
December 23, 1943	Appointed to command 21 Army Group, England, in command of four Allied armies (2nd British, 1st and 3rd U.S., 1st Canadian) to invade France—the "Second Front."
June 6, 1944	D-Day landings, Normandy.
August 28, 1944	Allies capture Paris.
September 1, 1944	Promoted to field-marshal.
September 17–September 25, 1944	Battle of Arnhem.
December 17, 1944–January 16, 1945	Battle of the Ardennes.
March 23, 1945	21 Army Group crosses the Rhine, north of the Ruhr.
March 31, 1945	Eisenhower halts 21 Army Group race to Berlin.
May 4, 1945	NW German armed forces surrender unconditionally to Montgomery at Lüneburg.

Post–World War II

June 1945	Appointed commander in chief or British military governor of the British Zone of Occupation, Germany, and British member, Allied Control Commission, Berlin.

May 1, 1946	Appointed chief of the Imperial General Staff, London.
September 26, 1948	Appointed chairman, Western Union Commanders in Chief Committee, France.
April 1, 1951	Appointed deputy supreme commander, Supreme Headquarters Allied Powers Europe, Versailles, France (North Atlantic Treaty Organization).
September 1958	Retires after 50 years' soldiering, publishes memoirs.
March 24, 1976	Dies at Isington Mill, Alton, Hampshire.

MONTGOMERY

Soldier of a Waning Empire

F ROM HIS birth in England through his upbringing in Tasmania, Montgomery—"Monty"—was a misfit and black sheep, the third son of a gentle Anglican bishop and the bishop's handsome, younger, somewhat stupid and less-than-gentle, imperious wife.

Though his father wished him to enter the church, Monty—despite his almost bantam size (5′7″)—chose a military career, both at St. Paul's day school in London and at England's Royal Military College at Sandhurst. Reduced to the rank of cadet for near-fatal bullying, he "reformed" and was commissioned as an officer and soldier of empire in the Royal Warwickshire Regiment, becoming a subaltern in India before his battalion returned to England. As war became inevitable in the summer of 1914, Monty's battalion was first sent north to counter a possible German invasion there, then to France to help the French as part of the British Expeditionary Force.

That August Monty took part in a chaotic counterattack on the Germans in Belgium, followed by an even more calamitous British retreat from Mons, luckily avoiding capture. In October, as the German Schlieffen plan came to grief and Paris was saved, he took part in a more orderly British advance on Meteren, in Belgium, where he was so severely wounded that a grave was dug for him. Recuperating in England, he was denied permission to return to duty as a fighting soldier. Instead he was made a staff officer and put in charge of raising battalions of volunteer infantry soldiers; and he began to recognize a special calling.

Montgomery's service to the empire had required a mixture of ceremonial and policing duties, with occasional punitive sorties in the North-West Frontier of Afghanistan, such as that which Winston Churchill memorably described in *My Early Life* (1930). Trench warfare on the western front, however, was of a different nature— one in which men became cannon fodder as part of vast national armies slugging it out against fellow Europeans for mere yards of muddy, artillery-obliterated soil. Winston Churchill, resigning as First Sea Lord after the debacle in the Dardanelles, commanded an infantry battalion in the months before the great Battle of the Somme in 1916—and warned the British Cabinet against such an approach to modern warfare. Without effective control of the generals, however, the mass, industrialized killing was permitted by the politicians to continue—a veritable holocaust in which, at the Somme, some six hundred thousand British, British empire, and French casualties were sustained in a massive, frontal assault ordered by Field-Marshal Haig, which never advanced more than three kilometers.

As a brigade-major, and later as an increasingly senior operations officer at corps headquarter level, and finally as chief of staff of an infantry division in the field, Montgomery took part in many of the bloodiest battles of World War I, from the Somme to Passchendaele and the German Spring Offensive. His earlier insubordination and bullying became subsumed in a ruthless professionalism—a determination to master the art of modern warfare against the most militaristic nation in the world at that time. And the secret of success, Montgomery recognized, was in rehearsal.

Planning offensive operations that were within the capability of volunteer troops, backed by coordinated artillery, became Montgomery's forté. His simplifying, almost mathematical mind saw the world in black and white; his sins of omission (failure to pay deference to superiors he despised, lack of interest in life outside soldiering) did not count against him in a war of attrition. The more frightened they were by noise, death, and the absolute destruction of everything around them, the more Montgomery's men increasingly put their trust in him, because he seemed so confident in himself and determined to make their tasks achievable. As Monty put his views in a private letter to home, after visiting his older brother at the headquarters of a Canadian formation struggling to advance more than a few yards at Passchendaele, "At plain straightforward fighting they are magnificent, but they are narrow minded and lack soldierly instincts"; for as soldiers, the Canadians had yet to learn that "the whole art of war is to gain your objective with as little loss [of life] as possible."[1]

Serving in the Anglo-French retreat during the German Spring Offensive in 1918 and then in the Allied counteroffensive which eventually forced the Germans to agree to an armistice, Montgomery emerged, at age thirty-one, a brilliant, decorated staff officer and temporary lieutenant-colonel who had experience of almost every form of infantry warfare save amphibious invasion. That too, in time, would come.

Without the advent of World War II, Montgomery, like Winston Churchill, would have gone down in history as a failure—both men considered by their colleagues and superiors to be talented mountebanks: selfish, vain, arrogant, and impossible to work with.

Both Churchill and Montgomery had been educated at the Royal Military College at Sandhurst, and had had their first lessons in soldiering on the North-West Frontier between India and Afghanistan. Thereafter, however, their approaches to warfare parted. Churchill, as the grandson of a duke, was a romantic imperialist and cavalryman, guided by a lingering Victorian dream of empire; Montgomery, the grandson of a British lieutenant-governor of the Punjab and a social misfit, struggling with barely controlled homosexual desires, identified with the Indians as a conquered people. Moreover he learned to despise the white "servants" of Churchill's beloved empire: the socially snobbish, professionally indolent, harddrinking, hunting-and-fishing "regular" army officers who forbade "shop talk" at the mess table, swapped wives, and saw soldiering as a game.

Montgomery's experience fighting the Germans in World War I taught him that traditional British approaches to empire and to war were obsolete. Yet to his astonishment they were allowed, like the English class system, to revive and reestablish themselves. At the Staff College in Camberley—to which Monty gained acceptance in 1920—it was, for instance, considered a punishment to have to sit beside Montgomery at breakfast and have to converse about . . . warfare! In fact, Montgomery spent the next twenty years on the edge of dismissal for insubordination, or forced early retirement, because of his lack of "social graces."

Yet within this moribund British army—which threw out Captain Basil Liddell-Hart, the architect of armored warfare—Monty himself remained loyal to the people who counted: his men. He was always the first officer to be sent to "hot spots," such as the Irish "Troubles" in 1921–22 and Palestine in 1937–38, for his ruthless professionalism brooked no compromise or weakness in dealing with insurrection. Yet even there his independence of mind kept him open to larger considerations. While his fellow veteran of the Irish "Troubles," Maj. A. E. Percival (later Lieutenant-General Percival, who surrendered Singapore to the Japanese without firing a shot), felt that the British had made a terrible mistake in leaving southern Ireland at a moment when they could have "crushed" the rebels, Montgomery felt otherwise. "My own view is that to win a war of that sort you must be ruthless," he wrote back; "Oliver Cromwell, or the Germans, would have settled it in a very short time. Nowadays public opinion precludes such methods; the nation would never allow it, and the politicians would lose their jobs if they sanctioned it. That being so I consider that Lloyd George was really right in what he did [granting independence to Eire]; if we had gone on we could probably have squashed the rebellion as a temporary measure, but it would have broken out like an ulcer the moment we had removed the troops; I think the rebels would probably have refused battle, and hidden away their arms, etc., until we had gone. The only way therefore was to give them some form of self-government, and let them squash the rebellion themselves; *they* are the only people who could really stamp it out."[2]

It was this realism, running hand-in-hand with his own relentless professionalism, that made Montgomery such an unusual soldier in Britain in the interwar period. His dedication to the art of training, though ignored by most military historians after World War II, was in retrospect almost incredible—indeed in many ways would save his country, for it was in the two decades between 1919 and 1939 that he developed and rehearsed what he considered the best approach to soldiering for a democratic nation: the formation of a cadre of professional officers, noncommissioned officers, and enlisted men who were trained with skills and knowledge that would allow them, in turn, to train volunteers and conscripts in the event that the country mobilized for war.

Training, in Monty's view, had nothing to do with ceremony and everything to do with personnel management, planning ahead, rehearsal, teaching lessons, cooperation among different types of units—in other words, professionalism. As the American military historian Carlo D'Este would write, "'Monty' was not cut from the same cloth as most other British officers"—yet he would be mistakenly caricatured as one by those who disliked him. Such critics had little notion of Monty's long preparation for high command. He was not interested in drill among reservists—"any high standard of drill in the Territorial army [reservists] is almost impossible and it is really [a] waste of time to try and obtain it," he cautioned his contemporary, Liddell Hart. What he wanted was simply to "get rid of that 'sloppy' look" and then concentrate on what was vital: "tactical training."[3]

For Montgomery, training in peacetime was a mental challenge; how could he make soldiers become interested in realistic, tactical problems they might one day have to face in battle? He therefore developed a style of "exercises" in which he presented scenarios in a contemporary setting and rehearsed tactical ways of dealing with them so that, in the event of actual hostilities, officers and men would never be surprised or lack professional confidence in being able to deal with the situation. Already in 1925 he was positing, for the purpose of tactical exercises in his regiment, the invasion of Britain by a swiftly re-arming enemy—eight years before Hitler successfully came to power in Germany. Intimate cooperation between infantry and artillery, the ability to fight at night, and air force cooperation were all practiced by his men. Thirteen years later, in 1938, he had not let up, but was mounting a similar operation, only on a larger scale, involving warships, aircraft, and tanks to rehearse both meeting an invasion and launching an invasion.

Would that the commanders of Britain's failed invasion of Norway in 1940 had paid heed! Instead, colleagues and superiors mocked Monty's seeming obsession with training and preparation for modern warfare—especially those who felt that modern war would be swiftly won by weaponry such as tanks and aircraft provided they were designed and manufactured in time to meet the burgeoning Nazi menace. For Monty, such cavils missed the point. Weapons could and would constantly be improved; but the men who fought with such weaponry, he felt, must "know their stuff," the stuff being tactics and communications—and it was his job, he reckoned, to teach them.

Thus, as the situation deteriorated between Germany and Poland in late August 1939, and another world war appeared inevitable, Montgomery, peremptory and unyielding, became perhaps the least liked senior officer in the British army but his country's greatest trainer of men. The situation nearly became a calamity when, with partial mobilization put into effect in Britain, Montgomery—having successfully put down an Arab insurrection in Palestine—was placed in a pool of unemployed generals!

Only on August 28, 1939, six days before Britain's declaration of war against Nazi Germany, was Monty at last given command of a regular division in England: the 3rd (Iron) Division, which would be one of the first British formations to be sent to France as part of the new British Expeditionary Force if war again broke out as it had in August 1914.

On September 3, 1939, with Hitler rejecting an ultimatum to pull back his forces invading Poland, war was duly declared by Britain, then by France. This time, at least, Bernard Montgomery would embark for France as a major-general—not a junior lieutenant.

Dunkirk

P OLAND WAS conquered by German forces in a few weeks, thanks to a non-aggression pact made between the Third Reich and the Soviet Union in the spring of 1939. Elated, Hitler ordered plans to be drawn up for a German attack on the western European nations that had, in support of Poland, dared declare war on the Reich—and even on those, like Holland and Belgium, which had not.

In the event, the Third Reich found it impossible to mount a Wehrmacht offensive on the scale necessary for crushing the French that fall, and this afforded the Allies time to analyze and take into account German methods of assault used in the Polish campaign. That the French and British did nothing to prepare their forces beyond digging into the Maginot Line and approving a cockeyed scheme to rush their forces north into unreconnoitered riverline positions in neutral Belgium once Hitler launched his expected invasion of the west remains one of the greatest military blunders of the twentieth century.

In the circumstances Monty, having experienced the retreat from Mons in 1914 and the Allied fall-back during Ludendorff's bloody Spring Offensive in 1918, was cruelly realistic about the Allies' chances of holding back German armored forces. French morale, he noted on his visits to neighboring French divisions, was completely defeatist, while the British Expeditionary Force was commanded by an English lord who had won the Victoria Cross for gallantry in World War I, but was completely out of his depth commanding a formation higher than a battalion—General Lord Gort. No rehearsals were ordered or conducted by Gort's headquarters, and the moment the Germans attacked on May 10, 1940, the British command structure became a farce. After the bombing of Rotterdam the Dutch surrendered without a further shot, while the Belgians shot into the air, then surrendered. The French armies meanwhile collapsed, allowing the German armored divisions to slice through the Ardennes and reach the English channel at Calais within days—cutting off the entire British Expeditionary Force (BEF) and remnants of the French forces that did not give in.

Winston Churchill, as the new prime minister, proposed a political union of France and Britain to keep up the struggle against the German assault in the West—but this was in part to compensate for the fact that, despairing of France's intentions to fight on, Churchill had refused to allow the Royal Air Force (RAF) to move its fighter squadrons to French soil. He pressed the BEF to counterattack the neck of the German armored salient, having no idea how modern German tactics had overwhelmed the Allies. With no hope of serious French resistance, the British were forced by events to authorize planning for the evacuation of the BEF from either Ostend or Dunkirk—to the consternation of the French government and high command.

Montgomery's performance as commander of a division, amid the debacle, was exemplary—and for interesting reasons, given Monty's later legendary performance as an army commander. In five great exercises in the winter months before Hitler's invasion, not only did he train his 15,000 men to move by night and fight by day, but he rehearsed them, in advance, in fighting retreat! As a result he brought almost his entire division back from the River Dyle in Belgium, through La Panne and Dunkirk, in an extraordinary display of cohesion, brilliant mobile communications, perfect artillery coordination, and iron command.

Promoted to temporary command of a corps, Montgomery was finally evacuated by destroyer on June 1, 1940, across the English Channel, defeated but unbowed. He had little idea that almost exactly four years later he would command the largest amphibious assault landing in human history, about a hundred miles to the south.

In 1927 Montgomery had married Mrs. Betty Carver, a World War I widow with two boys. Never a ladies' man, Monty had first proposed to a woman—in vain—at age thirty-seven, after one dance with a seventeen-year-old music student. But Betty Carver—the same age as Monty, and an artist—was different. That Monty was a misfit, she accepted. That he might be a military genius, she accepted. That he loved her, and her two boys, she was grateful. For ten years they did everything together. Betty even bore Monty a son, and when he took his infantry brigade on maneuvers in 1937, she rested nearby, in Devon, until they were over. Bitten by an insect on the beach, however, she fell ill with septicemia. This was in the days before penicillin or other antibiotics. First her leg became gangrenous and was amputated; then she died after several weeks of excruciating pain.

Monty was never the same thereafter—indeed his family attributed his iron self-discipline and absolute determination to "beat the Germans" to a barely sublimated anger over the death of his beloved wife.

Whether this was so must remain conjecture. It seems more likely that Montgomery, whose sexual orientation was otherwise directed exclusively towards men, had enjoyed in marriage a sort of respite from what was, in England, outlawed behavior and desire. Certainly he had never become romantically or physically close to any woman before courting his seventeen-year-old dance partner and then Betty, nor did he become so with any other woman for the rest of his life. If Montgomery did become more ruthless in his determination to save his country from military disaster, then, it was not so much *qua* grieving widower than as dedicated warrior, able to sublimate his love for young men at age fifty into perhaps the most extraordinary display of tactical and battlefield leadership in a democracy in the twentieth century.

In the interwar period, Monty had complained to a young

subordinate that during his entire five years on the western front in World War I, he had only ever seen the commander in chief of the BEF once! While contemporary commanders, in wars of armor, air power, and artillery, placed themselves in rear-headquarters from which they could shelter from enemy air attack and ensure the cooperation of different arms and services, Montgomery had advanced the notion of the battlefield tactical headquarters—or Tac HQ—a mobile communications center, often tented, from which the commander could visit his subordinate commanders and men, conducting the battle from the front rather than from the rear. Lord Gort had tried to create such a command post at the last moment during the German invasion of the West; it had been a complete disaster. What was crucial, Montgomery recognized, was rehearsal of command, and command communications, *before* battle.

It seems strange that this approach to modern battlefield command in a democratic nation in which the majority of combatants are volunteers or conscripted civilians would be so ignored by armchair historians—but the truth, as will be seen, is that Monty was in large part to blame for the underappreciation of his idea because he constantly engendered dislike by his insubordinate attitude.

Let us take an example. Disgusted by the performance of Lord Gort at Dunkirk, Monty demanded on his return to England an immediate interview with the new chief of the Imperial General Staff, General Dill—and told him that Lord Gort, his superior officer in the field, should be removed from field command and never employed again!

This was hardly the best way for a major-general to gain promotion, let alone another battlefield command. Instead Lord Gort himself was promoted to field-marshal, and the lessons of Dunkirk for the most part were ignored. It is hardly surprising, in retrospect, that it was another two years before Montgomery was finally given battlefield command again, as a lieutenant-general. In a post-Victorian/ Edwardian age his ability to rile his old-fashioned superiors— indeed, to reduce them to apoplectic rage—was second to none. When, having assumed the leadership of Britain on May 10, 1940, not only as prime minister but as self-appointed minister of defense,

Churchill inspected Montgomery's division on the south coast of England, a few weeks after Dunkirk, Monty unwisely boasted that, compared with the ageing prime minister (PM), he did not smoke, did not drink, and was a hundred percent fit.

Churchill eyed him wearily—and warily. "I drink, I smoke," the prime minister retorted with an undaunted smile, "*and I'm two hundred percent fit!*"[1]

Churchill's rhetoric, his refusal to surrender to or negotiate with Hitler, and his patient wooing of the American president, Franklin Delano Roosevelt, were three cardinal elements in Britain's survival—abetted by Hitler's mistakes.

There can be little doubt, in retrospect, that, had Hitler invaded Britain in the summer of 1940 without waiting to subdue the RAF, England would have fallen as swiftly as France. This was made clear to Churchill first when, as the First Sea Lord, he saw a lack of army, air, and naval cooperation doom his invasion of Norway in April 1940, then after he became prime minister, when the chaotic performance of the BEF brought failure at Dunkirk. Even Churchill cautioned his colleagues that wars are not won by evacuation—yet the actions of British forces across the globe in the twenty-four months thereafter, from 1940 to 1942, would leave a record of retreat, evacuation and capitulation, such as the surrender of the Tobruk garrison of 33,000 troops to Rommel on June 21, 1942. "Defeat is one thing," Churchill railed, "disgrace is another."[2]

In ceremony, the British army led the world; in skill and force, as defender of the free world, it had been outclassed by both Germans and Japanese.

The list of ignominious British defeats had become appallingly long. Commander after commander was appointed and then dismissed by Churchill, but the results did not improve. In Burma the British-led forces, under General Alexander, were forced to retreat to the very frontier of India; in North Africa, they were run back from Tripolitania to within sixty miles of Cairo and Alexandria. Indeed, the British Empire seemed to be crumbling—and with it, sadly, the future of democracy in a militaristic modern world run by dictators.

A stoic, taciturn lover of poetry, Gen. Sir Archibald Wavell, had been dismissed by Churchill as commander in chief in the Middle East in the summer of 1941 and replaced by Gen. Sir Claude Auchinleck. But if Wavell had been unable to deal with German forces, Auchinleck was even worse. Both of his appointees as 8th Army commanders in the desert proved broken reeds. In the struggle against Rommel's better armed, more mobile, and better trained African Panzer Army, pivoting on its famed Afrika Korps, the 8th Army simply fell apart—its polyglot British Empire units unable to coalesce into an effective fighting machine. By July 1942, diplomats and government agencies were burning their files in Cairo—indeed by August 1942 all of Auchinleck's senior headquarters staff had arranged for air evacuation to Palestine, in the event that Rommel broke through the last, forty-mile-wide major defensive position between the impassable sands of the Quattara Depression and the Mediterranean, an area named after a road and railway station known as El Alamein.

Though General Auchinleck had bravely taken personal command of the retreating 8th Army remnants and counterattacked in the Alamein area, in addition to his other duties in Cairo, this was but a temporary reprieve. The number of British Empire casualties in the desert that summer exceeded 100,000. It became questionable whether units and formations would continue to fight if they were continually and literally misled by the British high command. As the legendary commander of the South African Division, Gen. Dan Pienaar, expostulated on his field telephone, after being bombed by the RAF, "If you've got to bomb my trucks, you might at least hit them. But you missed every bloody one! See here. My father fought the British in the Transvaal, and all I want to know is, what side I'm supposed to be on now. Because if I'm on Rommel's side, say so, and I'll turn around and have him in Alexandria within twelve hours. Just work it out, and let me know as soon as you've decided."[3] The equally legendary commander of the New Zealand Division, Lt.-Gen. Bernard Freyberg, was even more disappointed by the lack of command at 8th Army headquarters. His division of 15,000 men had suffered 9,000 casualties—4,500 of them in July 1942 alone—

when Freyberg was himself wounded in the neck by a German shell. "The Army had for the moment disintegrated," he afterwards chronicled. "The system of command had broken down."[4]

Auchinleck's decision to break up the army into mobile battle groups and "jock columns" to deal with the enemy was "doomed to end in disaster against the Germans," Freyberg reflected.[5] Gen. Leslie Morshead—commander of the toughest of all the empire infantrymen, the Australian 9th Division—was driven almost to resign by the misuse of his beloved troops. Finally, the famous commander of the 4th Indian Division, Gen. "Gertie" Tuker, was equally contemptuous of the British high command. "I've never seen any sort of men, in any army or a football team, so sick at heart over their leadership as was the 8th Army" by the end of July 1942, he later wrote.[6] Few in the 8th Army believed "the Auk" had any hope of stopping Rommel from breaking through, as the Panzer Armee Afrika relentlessly summoned more men and matériel for the German-Italian *coup de grâce*.

It was at this point that the head of the British army, Gen. Sir Alan Brooke, decided to fly out to Egypt to see first-hand what was going wrong—for, as commander in chief of the Middle East, with his headquarters in Cairo, General Auchinleck was naturally in no position to criticize his own performance as commander of the 8th Army in the field, operating from a second headquarters at Alamein. The prime minister, despite his age and vulnerable health, then decided to accompany Brooke in a converted bomber, and see for himself what needed to be done, before flying on to visit Stalin in Moscow in the hope of convincing the communist dictator, despite the fact that German troops had reached the outskirts of Stalingrad, not to negotiate an armistice with Hitler.

Inspecting the 8th Army at Alamein on August 7, 1942, Churchill recognized with exasperation that the army would need yet another commander—its fourth in as many months. "I saw that army. It was a broken, baffled army, a miserable army. I felt for them with all my heart," Churchill later recorded—acknowledging as well his misgivings about General Auchinleck.[7] Auchinleck had ordered contingency plans to be drawn up for a full 8th Army retreat. Indeed when the former American presidential contender Wendell Willkie flew out to Egypt as President Roosevelt's personal emissary some days later, he was told it might be too late. "By the time we reached Khartoum, this speculation had become hard reports of what is known in Egypt as a 'flap'—a mild form of panic. In Cairo, some Europeans were packing cars for the flight southward or eastward. I recalled the President's warning to me just before I left Washington that before I reached Cairo it might well be in German hands. . . . The British Eighth Army was widely believed to be preparing to evacuate Egypt altogether, retiring to Palestine and southward into the Sudan and Kenya."[8]

Summoning his warlords—General Wavell from India, Field-Marshal Smuts from South Africa, General Wilson from Palestine—the prime minister, together with General Brooke, decided to replace the 8th Army commander for a fourth time, and his commander in chief in Cairo for a third time, substituting for Auchinleck his own favorite general, Sir Harold Alexander, the younger son of an earl, who had commanded a guards division in the final evacuation at Dunkirk before being sent to steer the British-led Indian army forces out of Burma—which was left to the Japanese to occupy. To serve under General Alexander the prime minister then personally chose Lieutenant-General Gott, a corps commander in the helter-skelter desert retreat from Tobruk, to take command of the beaten 8th Army.

It was a disastrous combination: two charming men, one without brains but with impeccable manners, the other brave but completely out of his depth, pessimistic, and exhausted. And both recovering from bitter retreat. The loss of Egypt, indeed possibly the entire Mediterranean, thus loomed, not despite Churchill's personal intercession, but because of it.

In retrospect, Churchill's mistake can be seen to have been one of the most parlous of World War II because, as historian Richard Overy has written, it is questionable whether the Soviets would have continued fighting if German forces had not only conquered Egypt but had pushed south from the Caspian Sea, brushed aside the forces of Gen. Maitland Wilson, cornered the remaining British in Palestine, and thus opened up "the prospect of German domination of the whole Middle East."[9]

Churchill might be a poor judge of men and a disaster-prone minister of defense, but he was nothing if not a great and wily strategist. To keep Russia in the war, the prime minister had already persuaded Roosevelt to overrule his American naval advisers and temporarily shelve any plans for the defeat of Japan in favor of committing the United States to a "Europe first" strategy—a two-step strategy that was tentatively scheduled to start with Allied landings in Vichy-French–controlled northwest Africa (Morocco and Algeria) in November that year. If Rommel conquered Egypt, however, and drove up into Palestine, would President Roosevelt follow through with the planned Anglo-American landings, for which he was still withholding the go-ahead? Malta, which was still defended by the British but whose population was now starving and whose meager forces were running out of ammunition, could not be resupplied by sea without air cover from airfields in Cyrenaica, recently captured intact by Rommel's Panzer army. If Rommel broke through to Cairo and Alexandria, not only Egypt but Malta, too, would fall—and with it, any hope of the Allies regaining naval control of the Mediterranean.

To many, British military incompetence seemed now to be of the same nature as that of France in the ominous early months of 1940: riddled with defeatism. The "chief reason why we are at a serious disadvantage compared with the Nazis over this business of the 'big ideas,'" a British Education Directorate booklet lamented at the time, "is that the evil things for which they [the Nazis] stand are novel and dynamic, whereas the excellent things for which we claim to be fighting may seem dull and uninspiring."[10]

This was the grotesque state of affairs when, shortly before Churchill was to emplane for Moscow at Heliopolis airfield, outside Cairo, the man the prime minister had personally appointed to command the 8th Army, Lieutenant-General "Strafer" Gott, was killed on his way back from Alamein, traveling illicitly (since he was neither sick nor wounded) in an air-ambulance. It was a godsend—or, as the prime minister himself acknowledged afterwards, a "blessing in disguise."

German Messerschmidt 109s, seeing the lumbering Bombay airplane lift off across the flat desert only a few miles across no-man's land at Alamein, had pounced, not only forcing the plane to crash-land, but setting it ablaze with passengers inside. It was cruel, but then war is cruel. What the pilots did not realize was that they had provided one of the greatest services that the Allies received in World War II.

In Cairo, the prime minister received the news with dismay. But to the relief of younger staff officers who despaired of the prime minister's poor military judgment, there was now a chance to appoint an *effective* 8th Army commander. Ignoring Churchill's personal dislike of Montgomery and preference for General "Jumbo" Wilson from Palestine, General Brooke once again pressed for Montgomery to be summoned from Home Forces in England to take command of the leaderless desert army.

Eventually, after much argument, Churchill caved in. A secret telegram was dispatched immediately to London. Monty's hour—indeed Britain's military hour—had come at last.

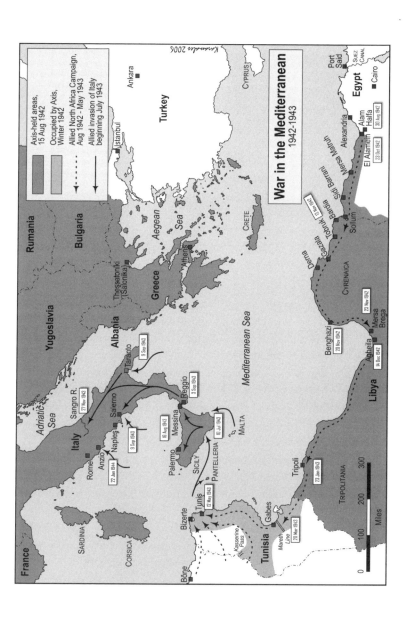

War in the Mediterranean
1942-1943

Legend:
- Axis-held areas, 15 Aug 1942
- Occupied by Axis, Winter 1942
- Allied North Africa Campaign, Aug 1942 - May 1943
- Allied invasion of Italy beginning July 1943

France

SARDINIA

CORSICA

Bône

Tunisia

Bizerte

Tunis — 12 May 1943

Kasserine Pass

Gabes

Mareth Line — 20 Mar 1943

Tripoli — 23 Jan 1943

TRIPOLITANIA

Libya

Agheila — 14 Dec 1942

Mersa Brega — 23 Nov 1942

Benghazi — 20 Nov 1942

CYRENAICA

Derna

Gazala

Tobruk — 13 Nov 1942

Bardia

Sidi Barrani

Sollum

Mersa Matruh

Alexandria

El Alamein — 23 Oct 1942

Alam Halfa — 30 Aug 1942

Egypt

Cairo

Port Said

SUEZ CANAL

PANTELLERIA

MALTA

SICILY

Palermo

Messina — 10 Jul 1943

16 Aug 1943

Reggio — 3 Sep 1943

Rome

Anzio — 22 Jan 1944

Naples

Salerno — 9 Sep 1943

Italy

Sangro R. — 27 Nov 1943

Taranto — 9 Sep 1943

Adriatic Sea

Yugoslavia

Albania

Rumania

Bulgaria

Greece

Athens

Thessaloniki (Salonika)

Aegean Sea

CRETE

Mediterranean Sea

Turkey

Ankara

Istanbul

CYPRUS

Miles
0   100   200   300

Kaminski 2006

Alamein

Montgomery's transformation of the beaten 8th Army would go down in history—for within two weeks of his arrival he defeated Rommel in major combat, in the Battle of Alam Halfa, which put paid to any danger of German breakthrough to Cairo and Palestine. Six weeks after that he launched one of the great Allied offensive battles of World War II: Alamein.

How did he do this? How in the space of such a short time did Montgomery instill a new ethos in a defeated British army and make it a household name throughout the free world?

It would become fashionable in the 1960s to downplay the Battle of Alamein as a World War I–style infantry and artillery battle in a desert theater that otherwise delighted military historians and battle-game players with its examples of spectacular tank maneuvering—like battle fleets operating on land. In doing so, however, they missed the crucial significance of the British victory. As one captured German general would remark, "The war in the desert ceased to be a game when Montgomery took over."[1]

German superiority in the desert was due to professionalism, co-operation among all arms, close air support, intelligence gathering—

and the quality of German tanks. German panzers, by 1942, had become justly celebrated for their reliability and firepower; no less than 200 of them sported new 75mm, long-barreled guns in their turrets, with frontal armor so thick no British or American artillery, let alone tank-gun, could pierce it. Moreover these Specials were backed by perhaps the most awesome ground-weapon of the war: a long-barreled German anti-aircraft gun on a simple mobile gun carriage that could hit and "kill" a tank faster than the speed of sound from a range of two miles; indeed it riddled targets at 16,000 yards. This was the German "88."

Blessed with an experienced *coup d'oeil militaire*, extraordinary leadership ability, and a sixth sense about enemy weakness, Rommel had run rings around the British in the desert, despite their larger numbers. Quality had proved more valuable than quantity. But in numbers also Rommel was building up a formidable arsenal for attack. By the end of August Field-Marshal Kesselring, the German commander in the Mediterranean, had one thousand German and Italian fighters and attack bombers to support Rommel's thrust to Cairo—including more than a hundred of the unmatchable Messerschmidt 109bf's.

It was imperative that, in taking over a broken army that had lost confidence in itself and had ceased to cohere, Montgomery slow down Rommel's naval-like mobile tactics. Traveling by car from Cairo to 8th Army headquarters on the Ruweisat Ridge two days before his official assumption of command, Monty was shaken by the atmosphere of hopelessness and the contingency plans for retreat. He therefore relieved the temporary commander, General Ramsden, on the spot; sent a rude message to Cairo saying 8th Army was under new management; and, having asked the entire headquarters staff to assemble at dusk, first set off to meet the men who would have to face Rommel's onslaught.

Montgomery's takeover and makeover of 8th Army was exemplified in the address he made to his new staff, outside his headquarters caravan, on the evening of August 13, 1942, the day he prematurely took command. After introducing himself, the white-kneed, sharp-nosed lieutenant-general outlined first the military situation as he saw it and then what he proposed to do about it.

> I do not like the general atmosphere I find here. It is an atmosphere of doubt, of looking back to select the next place to which to withdraw, of loss of confidence in our ability to defeat Rommel, of desperate defence measures by reserves in preparing positions in Cairo and the Delta.

"All that must cease," Monty ordered:

> Let us have a new atmosphere. The defence of Egypt lies here at Alamein and on the Ruweisat Ridge. What is the use of digging trenches in the Delta? It is quite useless; if we lose this position we lose Egypt; all the fighting troops now in the Delta must come here at once, and will. *Here* we will stand and fight; there will be no further withdrawal. I have ordered that all plans and instructions dealing with further withdrawal are to be burnt, and at once. We will stand and fight *here*. If we can't stay here alive, then let us stay here dead.

If Rommel attacked immediately, the situation would, he admitted, be awkward. But "if we have two weeks to prepare we will be sitting pretty; Rommel can attack as soon as he likes, after that, and I hope he does," the new Army commander declared—and went straight on to outline his ideas for 8th Army's *second* battle: a "great offensive" that would be "the beginning of a campaign that will hit Rommel and his Army for six right out of Africa."[2]

To plan for such a defensive, then offensive battle, the army staff would have to pull itself together and work hand-in-hand with the Royal Air Force (RAF). "This is a frightful place here, depressing and a rendez-vous for every fly in Africa," Monty remarked of 8th Army headquarters in what would become typical Monty-ese: a mix of schoolboy slang and absolute professional clarity of message. "We shall do no good here. Let us get over by the sea [alongside RAF headquarters] where it is fresh and healthy. If Officers are to do good work they must have decent messes, and be comfortable. So off we go on the new line."

As Montgomery finished the men stood up and saluted. They had heard one of the great military speeches of history, one that would prove to be a turning point in World War II. "One could have heard a pin drop if such a thing were possible in the sand in the desert," his new chief of staff, Brig. "Freddie" de Guingand, later recalled.

Certainly Monty's address presaged one the great reversals of morale to take place in a defeated army under new leadership. Summoning new commanding officers from Britain and sacking anyone who "bellyached," Montgomery laid down and rehearsed the plans for the British defensive battle of Alam Halfa—his preparations bolstered by the same Ultra intelligence (the highly-secret decoding of German signals at Bletchley Park in England) that the 8th Army had enjoyed before his arrival, throughout its months of failure and surrender.

At Alam Halfa, the 8th Army had new command and orders not to engage in mobile warfare, but rather to lure Rommel on to positions the British had prepared. Things were so different now that, from the moment his German and Italian tank forces breached the British minefields, Rommel knew in his heart of hearts he was in a trap—pounded night and day by the RAF, while the British artillery and tanks remained in their dug-in emplacements, refusing to be tempted into the gun sights of his two hundred 88mm and captured Russian 76.2mm mobile guns. "The swine isn't attacking!" Rommel complained to his "boss," Field-Marshal Kesselring.[3]

Monty wasn't—and he wouldn't until he was satisfied that his forces were good and ready. Wendell Willkie, visiting the 8th Army in the final stages of the battle, as Rommel admitted defeat and called off his offensive, was unreservedly admiring of Montgomery's professionalism, his self-confidence, and his rapport with his soldiers. "I was enormously impressed by the depth and thoroughness of General Montgomery's knowledge of his business. Whether it was corps or division, brigade, regiment, or battalion headquarters, he knew more in detail of the deployment of the troops, and location of the tanks than did the officer in charge. This may sound extravagant but it was literally true. The man's passion for detail is amazing."[4]

Some weeks later, on the eve of 8th Army's own offensive battle, timed to begin in moonlight in late October 1942, Montgomery issued his own variation on Nelson's famous signal before the Battle of Trafalgar. It was a "Personal Message from the Army Commander," to be read out to every one of the two hundred thousand soldiers who would be fighting in the battle.

When I assumed command of Eight Army, I said that the mandate was to destroy ROMMEL and his Army, and that it would be done as soon as we were ready.

We are ready NOW.

The battle which is about to begin will be one of the decisive battles of history. It will be the turning point of the war. The eyes of the whole world will be on us, watching which way the battle will swing.

We can give them their answer at once, "It will swing our way."

We have first-class equipment; good tanks; good anti-tank guns; plenty of artillery and plenty of ammunition; and we are backed up by the finest air striking force in the world.

All that is necessary is that each one of us, every officer and man, should enter the battle with the determination to see it through— to fight and to kill—and finally to win.

If we all do this, there can be only one result—together we will hit the enemy for six—right out of North Africa.

The sooner we win this battle, which will be the turning point of the war, the sooner we shall all get back home to our families.

Therefore, let every officer and man enter the battle with a stout heart, and with the determination to do his duty so long as he has breath in his body.

AND LET NO MAN SURRENDER SO LONG AS HE IS
UNWOUNDED AND CAN FIGHT.[5]

In the early hours of October 24, 1942, 8th Army launched a concentrated attack on Rommel's line at Alamein with an infantry trained to advance in darkness through half a million mines, and with the greatest artillery barrage since World War I stunning the enemy in its dugout positions. New American tanks, landed at Suez in September, had replaced the largely worn-out British armor. In addition, American bomber and bomber-escort squadrons now operated alongside the RAF. But what Willkie had witnessed before the arrival of such additional weaponry—as had Churchill on his way back from Moscow—was a transformation of morale and a new spirit at work, a professionalism that seemed to ripple through the army under its new commander. It was an infectious confidence in victory that did, indeed, carry the 8th Army through to the end at Alamein despite grueling conditions, setbacks, and ubiquitous German armor and anti-tank weapons.

From the moment he arrived in the desert, Montgomery had begun to retrain 8th Army as a whole. His predecessors had had access to Ultra, but had used such intelligence only to gain tactical advantages (for example, identifying Italian units, which were easier to attack than German ones). Battles, as opposed to skirmishes, could not be won by intelligence, however. Intelligence must be used to ensure the best chance of success for retrained, well-rehearsed troops working to fulfill a master battle plan—his plan. At the defensive battle of Alam Halfa Montgomery had proved to his own troops that his methods worked. In the bloody, twelve-day Battle of Alamein, his troops—Englishmen, Highlanders, South Africans, Indians, Rhodesians, Australians, New Zealanders, Greek, Free French—proved in battle that they would follow him to the death.

In the British army, at least, such cohesive international cooperation was a wholly new phenomenon. In his prebattle talks to all senior officers, *even* including lieutenant-colonels, he had predicted a three-part battle—the massive surprise "break-in"; the long "dog-fight" that would wear down an enemy trying desperately to seal off the penetration; and the "break" of the enemy—warning them "not to expect results too soon."[6] Sadly, because no significant American units were involved in Egypt beyond bombers and escort fighters, senior American military personnel were not present to appreciate the sheer magnitude of Montgomery's achievement when, on November 4, 1942, Rommel's remnants fled from Alamein, leaving more than thirty thousand troops to be captured. Thus, when, at a teach-in shortly after the capture of Tripoli in February 1943, Montgomery attempted to pass on the lessons of his experience in fighting Rommel, American officers were put off by Monty's British boastfulness and know-it-all air. General Patton, for example, attending the conference after his successful invasion of Morocco at Casablanca, was derisive. "I may be old, I may be slow, and I may be stoopid," he told Monty's best armored corps commander, Gen. Brian Horrocks, "but it don't mean a thing to me."[7]

Once Rommel's panzers broke through at Kasserine a few days later, however, even Patton was forced to eat his words. Fighting the Germans, American commanders realized, was nowhere near as easy as it looked.

Rommel himself appreciated Montgomery's superiority in command skills, as did General von Thoma, his Afrika Korps commander, a veteran of the Russian front who was captured on the last day of the Battle of Alamein. The Germans might have better-made weapons and superior tactical skills, thanks to their more flexible, less hidebound approach to training and professional performance. But, von Thoma felt, with greater potential resources the Allies needed only to learn to marshal their forces under effective leaders to win, ultimately. "In modern mobile warfare, the tactics are not the main thing," he pointed out. "The decisive factor is the organization of one's resources—to maintain momentum."[8]

This, Monty had done. Yet his cautiousness in the desert struck von Thoma as strange, given the Allies' superiority in numbers. This typically militaristic German simply failed to understand what Montgomery was up against in the old-fashioned, democratic English imperial class structure—especially the lack of training and rehearsal prior to major operations of war. Even sixty years later, almost no British or American military history or biography relating to World War II would list "training" in its index. Combined with the sheer amateurishness of the British approach to war on land, poorly designed and poorly made British equipment had formed a monumental challenge which Montgomery, arriving fresh out of England, had had to reverse on the very field of battle.

The same failure to understand the magnitude of Britain's military problem, sadly, would initially be true among American echelons, where rivalry and cultural differences between American and British personnel led to mutual disparagement. Thus after General Eisenhower met Montgomery in the desert (only his second meeting with him—and on the first occasion, in England, Eisenhower had been rudely told to stop smoking while Monty gave a lecture), he noted in a letter to his boss, Army Chief of Staff General Marshall, that Monty "is unquestionably able, but very conceited." Indeed, Eisenhower went so far as to say that General Montgomery "is so proud of his successes to date that he will never willingly make a single move until he is absolutely certain of success—in other words, until he has concentrated enough resources so that anybody could practically guarantee the outcome."[9]

After three years of unending British defeat in the war against Hitler's forces, this was *exactly* Monty's approach: to try to guarantee victory by means of proper training and rehearsal. Certainly, previous efforts to overcome the Germans with anything less than overwhelming resources had resulted only in failure and was doing so in Algeria and Tunisia at that very moment, however much Eisenhower might wish it to be otherwise.

Eisenhower's attitude was due in part to the innocence of an American commander in chief in unfamiliar territory (Africa). But it also reflected a major difference between American and British attitudes towards war on land. American commanders and troops would certainly demonstrate an amazing ability to rebound from reverse and defeat; but after three long years of defeats at German and Japanese hands, from Norway to Egypt and Singapore, British and British

Dominion troops, Montgomery knew, wanted the assurance of victory if they laid down their lives—and Monty therefore refused to undertake offensive operations unless he was certain they were within the capability of his men.

Montgomery's stubborness in this respect was soon tested to the limit. At Casablanca, as the war in northwest Africa neared its end, it was decided that the next step in the war effort of the western Allies would be an amphibious landing on the island of Sicily, which would give them more control of the Mediterranean skies and a jumping-off point for an Allied landing on the mainland of Italy—the threat of which would force an Italian surrender and keep German divisions in the Mediterranean, away from the coast of northern France. Eisenhower's staff thereupon drew up plans for a series of small amphibious landings, over five days, along the 600-mile coast of Sicily.

Monty was aghast. As far back as 1927, in a series of articles on tactics in military history for his regimental journal, he had emphasized the shortcomings of such an approach:

> All through history, from the days of the great phalanx of the Roman Legion, the master law of tactics remains unchanged; this Law is that to achieve success you must be superior at the point where you intend to strike the decisive blow.[10]

Dispersion of effort had already been the downfall of the British 8th Army in the desert against Rommel in 1941 and 1942. Indeed only by transferring the 8th Army's best troops, including Montgomery's armor, to Eisenhower's Tunisian front had the Allies been able to finish the campaign in North Africa, in May 1943, with a final, decisive attack on Tunis. Now, less than a month after applying decisive, concentrated force in Tunisia, the Allies were hoping to invade Sicily in penny-packets that could easily be sealed off and pushed back into the sea by swift German reactions. Rightly or wrongly, Montgomery flatly refused to carry out the plan as 8th Army commander. "I should say he was good probably on the political line," Monty had remarked privately of Eisenhower, "but obviously knows nothing whatever about fighting"[11]—an opinion he never really changed. (The American general Omar Bradley held similar views.

"[Eisenhower's] African record clearly demonstrates he did not know how to manage a battlefield," Bradley wrote later.[12])

After having been compelled to remove his own U.S. II Corps commander, General Fredendall, following the American defeat at Kasserine, and temporarily replace him with Gen. George S. Patton, Eisenhower did, however, have the wisdom to put the American part of the Sicilian operation in the charge of someone who knew about fighting the Germans: Patton. Fredendall had attempted to direct his corps from a specially-constructed bunker sixty miles behind the front; General Patton, like Montgomery, wanted to inspire his troops, and he led from the front.

Monty and Patton

Belatedly canceling his plans for widely dispersed landings on Sicily, Eisenhower reluctantly accepted Montgomery's plan to land a single, overwhelming Allied force at its southeastern tip, with ample air and sea cover.

Operation Husky, the invasion of Sicily on July 10, 1943, was the greatest amphibious assault of the war in terms of initial assault strength: eight divisions assaulting in a concentrated *Schwerpunkt*, or decisive point, on the southeast coast of the island, between Syracuse and Licata. As a dress rehearsal of the Allies' capability to launch an invasion by air, sea, and ground, it was stunningly successful; yet Eisenhower's decision to divide the eight assaulting divisions into two armies under the overall command of General Alexander, though a political success, proved a military mistake. General Patton, commanding the new 7th U.S. Army, emphasized quick, forceful advances made by armored equipment; General Montgomery, commanding 8th British Army, emphasized well-marshaled forces and masterful technique. Together, they could have formed a perfect duo—but harnessing two such thoroughbreds would have required the presence in the field of a kind of commander in chief the allies did not have. Sadly, neither Alexander—whom Eisenhower had appointed to be his deputy and ground force commander—nor General Eisenhower himself, was that man.

Both Patton and Montgomery liked the charming Gen. Sir Harold Alexander as a person but despised him as a tactician. The main German forces were currently pinned down in a bloody battle in the plain of Catania, but instead of smashing his way around the German right, Patton requested and won permission from Alexander to send his armor racing in the opposite direction, to Palermo, on the western tip of the island, in a mission that his deputy, General Bradley, called "meaningless in a strategic sense"[1] and that the official American historian contemptuously termed "a publicity agent's stunt."[2] This caused the 7th U.S. Army to miss a chance to cut off the German forces facing Patton's own U.S. II Corps and 8th Army. Without such flanking forces, Monty meanwhile found himself facing even tougher opposition than that which he had faced in North Africa. As additional high-grade German ground troops parachuted in, they established themselves in echelons in this land seemingly designed for defense, with stonewalled olive groves stretching back to Mount Etna, which offered them a clear view not only of the Catanian plain but even of the sea approaches to the Messina Strait, which divides Sicily from the mainland and was thus their chosen escape route. Foreseeing the German actions, Montgomery had begged to be allowed to command the whole battle of Sicily, with both American corps under his 8th Army command, so that, if they were countered on one flank, he could hold the German forces there while reinforcing success on his left flank, as he had done in the Battle of Mareth in North Africa.

Monty's victory at Mareth, in March 1943, had, after all, demonstrated his great ability to adapt his battle plan to circumstances—for example, General Horrocks's left-flanking hook, launched out of the evening sun to the west of Mareth, brought a brilliant victory to 8th Army after its bloody failure trying to breach the main Mareth line.[3]

In Sicily, however, the Allies had allowed their land forces to be divided by nation, with a commander in chief too far away, in Algiers, to take charge, and a deputy, General Alexander, nominally in charge of the land battle, but too compliant and fundamentally indolent to make the necessary tactical decisions. A combination of punitive main attack and mobile, outflanking movement on the western wing, after a brilliant surprise landing, could have brought a great Allied victory in Sicily—as it would do, finally, in Normandy. But in Sicily it was not to be.

Disheartened by Alexander's failure to "grip" the tactical strategy required for such a campaign, Monty was deeply disappointed in the Allied command set-up, especially the separation between the various service headquarters. Eisenhower's own headquarters remained at Algiers; General Alexander's was in Malta, then Syracuse; Air Marshal Tedder's was in Tunis; and the Allied naval commander, Admiral Cunningham, was headquartered in Malta.

Although the British chiefs of staff sent a message on June 17, 1943, to warn Eisenhower of their "concern" that the three army, air, and naval commanders would not be sharing the same headquarters ("In our view separation of HQs of one commander from that other two violates one of the most important principles of Combined Operations"[4]), Eisenhower did nothing to correct the situation, and as a result the Germans were permitted by both the Allied navies and the air forces to evacuate their entire Sicilian army to the mainland by mid-August 1943. As American historian Carlo D'Este has written, 60,000 Germans had managed to hold back 450,000 Allied troops for thirty-eight days—and to get away, almost to a man.[5] "It beats me how anyone thinks you can run a campaign in that way, with each of the three Commanders of the three services about 600 miles from each other," Monty lamented in his diary.[6]

Worse, however, was to follow. Monty had written to Field-Marshal Brooke, the chief of the Imperial General Staff in London, to suggest that the Allies launch their promised cross-Channel invasion that year, while the Germans were focused (as Churchill had promised Stalin would be the case) on the Mediterranean. Brooke and Churchill, however, became absolutely determined to make mainland Italy—the "soft underbelly" of Hitler's conquered Europe—into a primary theater of war, rather than simply keep Axis divisions there facing a permanent Allied threat, as was the case in German-occupied Norway. Thus while Patton was severely reprimanded and withdrawn from combat for slapping and then drawing his gun to threaten shell-shocked 7th U.S. Army soldiers in a Sicilian field hospital, Monty was ordered to brush up on his Italian. To invade mainland Italy would be 8th Army's next task, Brooke decided.

Decades later the popular American image of Montgomery would be molded by a 1969 Academy Award–winning film, *Patton*, in which Montgomery in Sicily was caricatured as "a buffoon," to use D'Este's words,[7] attempting to steal Patton's glory by ensuring that his British troops reached Messina before American troops could get there. Nothing could have been more historically untrue. While Patton certainly urged his American troops to be the first into the city, and almost ended his career with the unfortunate "slapping incident," Montgomery had specifically arranged three weeks *before* the capture of the city, at a personal conference at Syracuse on July 25, for Patton to seize Messina with his 7th U.S. Army troops—only too pleased for the Americans to take over more of the fighting from his exhausted 8th Army divisions, whose trials, on the mainland of Italy, were only now to begin.

As Carlo D'Este has written, the campaign on mainland Italy was another Churchillian mistake: a campaign that would cause the forces of some sixteen nations to become "mired in a war of attrition that was utterly without strategic purpose and which dragged on until May 1945, resulting in the heaviest losses of any campaign fought by the western Allies in World War II."[8]

Protesting to no avail, Montgomery did his duty—lamenting that Operation Baytown, a crossing of the Messina Straits by the 8th Army, and subsequent operations in the "boot" of Italy would be fatuous if the Allies were actually intending to land in force near Naples, hundreds of miles to the north.

Once again, neither Eisenhower nor Alexander seemed to have a strategic plan. "Before we embark on major operations on the mainland of Europe we must have a master plan and know how we propose to develop these operations," Monty complained. Instead, the 8th Army was ordered by Eisenhower to go ahead and cross the Messina Straits, which it did without difficulty on September 3, 1943—causing the Italian high command to agree secretly that day, in Sicily, to the surrender of all Italian armed forces not loyal to Mussolini (finally announced by the BBC on September 8). The main American-led landings were then conducted by Gen. Mark Clark's 5th U.S. Army, on September 9 at Salerno, south of Naples—but, with only a three-division assault across a thirty-six-mile front and with no preliminary naval or air bombardment, these very nearly proved a disaster.

Completely inexperienced in fighting the Germans, and even more inexperienced in dealing with his British allies, Gen. Mark Clark had allowed the British-controlled air force headquarters in North Africa to dictate where he could land—south of Naples, rather than at Gaeto, north of the great seaport. (Given the same orders with regards to the Husky operation, Montgomery had simply refused.) As a result Clark almost had to evacuate 5th Army, and the Germans learned that the next time a landing was attempted, their forces could simply race to the point of landing and cauterize it before it could break out.

The besetting sin of the Allies in fighting the Germans, Monty rued, was unwillingness to recognize the importance of overwhelming strength at the point of assault. This failure afforded the enemy, as ruthless professionals, every opportunity to take advantage of Allied amateurism, inexperience, slowness, and incoherence. Thus, when the Allies came to launch their next amphibious assault in Italy in January 1944, it should have been no surprise that the result proved even worse than Salerno—an entire American-British Corps held on the beachhead for *five months*!

Like operations in Gallipoli in the Dardanelles, Operation Shingle was the brainchild of Winston Churchill—who, once again, had gone to the Mediterranean to be "the man on the spot." But more damaging still than his management of Operation Shingle itself ("a stranded whale" instead of "a tiger," as Churchill later snarled), however, was his determination to appoint his favorite general, Sir Harold Alexander, as the commander in chief of the Allied land armies in Overlord, the all-important cross-Channel invasion of France, set for the summer of 1944.

Overlord

"WHO WILL command Overlord?" Stalin had challenged Churchill and President Roosevelt at the summit meeting in Tehran in late November 1943. Roosevelt and Churchill had both blushed, for they had appointed no one—only a junior staff general, "Freddie" Morgan, was in charge of planning a possible landing in France.

General Marshall, in Washington, and General Brooke, in London, each assumed he would be named supreme commander for the second front. Some days later, however, on December 7, 1943, Roosevelt asked General Eisenhower to assume the mantle—despite his lackluster performance in Sicily and Italy (his headquarters were still in Algiers—two years after his landing in Algeria!). Though Eisenhower, as Allied commander in chief, had made but two visits to Italy since the invasion of the Italian mainland four months before, he was selected by President Roosevelt for his "battlefront knowledge," according to Eisenhower's diarist. Roosevelt's son James, however, knew better. In answer to a question by James as to why he had picked Eisenhower over General Marshal, Roosevelt had confided, "Eisenhower is the best politician among the military men."[1]

Eisenhower, flattered by the historic role, duly asked for Gen. Sir Harold Alexander to be his "single ground commander." Churchill was delighted, and ready to acquiesce immediately—but, as with the decision to appoint General Gott to command the 8th Army at Alamein, fate fortunately decided otherwise. Felled by an attack of pneumonia, Churchill was forced to spend December recuperating in the Mediterranean and North Africa, leaving the British Labour Party leader and deputy prime minister, Clement Attlee, in charge of the government in England. Mr. Attlee had been a major on the western front in World War I, and as a dedicated socialist had qualms about appointing the son of an earl to command the crucial Second Front, on which proletarian Russian hopes were pinned. Sir Harold Alexander, it was true, had taken part in a famous school cricket match between Harrow—Churchill's old school—and Eton (Fowler's Match); he also had impeccable manners that impressed Churchill, the grandson of a duke and a somewhat fawning monarchist. But Alexander did not impress Deputy Prime Minister Attlee—who, on behalf of the British Cabinet and in consultation with General Brooke, directed the secretary of state for war to inform Churchill that, if the affable Eisenhower was going to be supreme commander instead of the tough, no-nonsense General Marshall, then the Allied land force commander had better be a tough, no-nonsense commander, if the Germans were to be defeated.

Thus it was that, on December 23, 1943, Montgomery received the news by secret cipher that, as Allied ground force commander, he would be leading the Allied armies in the greatest invasion in history: D-Day.

In Algiers, Eisenhower, disappointed that General Alexander's name had been turned down, nevertheless confirmed to Montgomery that he wanted him to "take complete charge of the land battle," while Eisenhower himself would ensure the unity of air, naval, and military forces. Both were agreed that the current outline plan for Overlord, which called for a three-divisional assault like that at Salerno, was nonsense—and that, even if it meant delaying the landings, there had to be a bigger punch on D-Day. In Marrakesh, Churchill then handed Monty his own copy of the latest version of the top secret detailed plans for Overlord, drawn up by a committee that had been working on the invasion scheme for over a year under the chief of staff to the supreme Allied commander-designate (COSSAC).

Monty told Churchill frankly that he was appalled by the plan. General Morgan's COSSAC plan vitiated, in his view, every principle of effective combat against the Germans. As Montgomery explained to the prime minister, Morgan's idea was to land only three divisions on a narrow front at Arromanches, in Normandy, under an American commander whose job would be to seize Caen; then for the British 21 Army Group commander to take over, in the middle of the battle, and organize the troops into two armies—one American, one Canadian—under his command. The Canadian army, on the left flank of the invasion force, would make for Paris, while on the right, the American army would make for Cherbourg after about a month's fighting—splitting off an echelon to strike down to Brittany as it did so. It was, in Monty's parlance, "a dog's breakfast."

Assuring Churchill that he had Eisenhower's full permission to stir things up, Monty flew on to London to confront the planners. Summoning the COSSAC team on January 3, 1944, to the 21 Army Group headquarters in his old school in West London, St. Paul's, he made both staffs give him a personal presentation of their plans and the reasoning behind them. Then he responded to their proposals.

The notion of landing in Normandy—rather than crossing the English Channel at its narrowest point and trying to seize one of the French ports at Calais or Boulogne—was a sensible idea, he acknowledged, since the Germans had a complete panzer army sitting in the Pas de Calais and very few troops in Normandy or Brittany. To imagine, however, that Hitler would sit back and watch first an American-led army, then a Canadian-led army charge straight from the beaches to Caen and on to Paris without counterattacking them with his armored forces was idle fantasy. Monty then detailed the problems he had already pointed out to the prime minister: only three divisions landing on the first day of assault, on too narrow a front, with subsequent divisions following through a "fatally congested" beachhead—all making for too many simultaneous destinations, with a ridiculously complicated command set-up, and the wrong tactical strategy for the subsequent battle.

Simplicity was the cardinal element in modern fighting, Monty emphasized—for without it the fog of war simply enveloped an operation or campaign. He knew this because he had seen it happen so many times, both in the last war and in the current one. What the Allies must do, he told the planning team as the new Allied land forces commander, was not become fixated on Caen and Paris, but first seize the port of Cherbourg, on the Cotentin peninsula. Cherbourg must be the primary, not subsidiary, Allied objective. As American forces did this, it would be the job of the British and Canadian forces on the eastern flank to bring to battle the main German forces streaming in from the Pas de Calais to attack the Allied bridgehead at their point of landing, drawing the Germans into combat at or south of Caen, Normandy's strategic road center.

Once Cherbourg was operational, in addition to the prefabricated floating Mulberry harbors the navy was planning to tow over (complete with breakwaters, docking caissons, and ramps onto the beaches), the Allies would build up their strength within the Allied bridgehead around Bayeux to the point where they had enough divisions to break out to the south, where the Germans were weakest—not to the north, where the Germans would be strongest, defending direct access to Paris and the Channel ports. In view of the importance of seizing Cherbourg as a first priority, Montgomery asked the planners why it wouldn't be feasible to land troops on the western side of the Cotentin/Cherbourg peninsula, in order to accelerate the port's capture—or at least, to land forces nearer Cherbourg, on the eastern side of the peninsula. Because of the urgency, he gave the staffs exactly twenty-four hours to respond.

The next day it was decided that for naval reasons, the western side of the peninsula must be ruled out for invasion, but the low-lying Cotentin marshland and beaches to the west of the proposed Arromanches area were considered perfectly assault-friendly, if assault craft for more troops could be landed on day one. Monty promised he would make this a priority in his signals to Eisenhower in

Washington—and went off to inspect his new American troops in 1st U.S. Army, as their new invasion commander.

To those who had witnessed Montgomery's takeover in the desert in August 1942, the situation in London early in January 1944 was uncannily familiar. On his arrival in the desert Monty had thrown out existing plans for dispersed columns working on their own and had ordered the destruction of all contingency plans for retreat, making clear how he would fight Rommel, first in a defensive battle, then in a great offensive battle.

Now, a year and a half later, with Eisenhower's chief of staff to back him, he had assembled the huge Anglo-American planning staffs for Overlord—and in three days he transformed a recipe for failure into a clear, simple plan for Allied success.

There was one further similarity between the situations at Alamein and at Normandy: the ground commanders facing each other across the English Channel. In December 1943, under the supreme command of Field-Marshal Gerd von Runstedt, Hitler had appointed Field-Marshal Erwin Rommel to be commander of Army Group B, responsible for the defense of the coastline of German-occupied northern France and Belgium.

Once again, Monty would thus face Rommel, this time across the often stormy waters of the English Channel instead of a desert sewn with Rommel's landmines, or "devil's gardens"—though these, too, nicknamed "Rommel's asparagus" (mined anti-tank and anti–landing craft obstacles), soon began to spring up on the former tourist beaches of the French coast, as Rommel tirelessly toured the "Atlantic Wall."

Both Montgomery and Rommel were aware that, as in August 1942, they were in a race against time. The Battle of Alamein, Monty had predicted while planning his offensive in the fall of 1942, would take twelve days and nights of unrelenting, bitter fighting—and it had, to the day. With ten times as many troops, Monty predicted in January 1944, D-Day and the battle of Normandy would take almost ten times as long—ninety days, he calculated. All effort must therefore be made to ensure that the invasion would kick off in May, to afford the Allied armies ample summer weather for the campaign.

General Bradley, who had been commanding 1st U.S. Army in England since September 1943, listened to Monty's new plans at a meeting of commanders at St. Paul's School on January 7, 1944, and was delighted—especially when Montgomery explained that the Anglo-Canadian 2nd British Army, landing on the left side of the all-American 1st U.S. Army, would have as its main purpose to strike out towards Caen and would thereafter "operate to the south to prevent any interference with the American army from the East." Caen would thus be a "hinge," Bradley's chief planner recalled. The objective of the 1st U.S. Army was quite clear from the outset, namely "the capture of Cherbourg and the clearing of the Cherbourg peninsula. They [the Americans] will then develop operations to the south [the Loire] and west [Brittany]."[2]

Such explicitness and simplicity thrilled Bradley—who had felt that "with our existing resources" and against the "strength of enemy forces in North-West Europe" the COSSAC plan for Overlord was simply "impractical."[3]

As at Alamein, Monty's take-over of the D-Day operation two weeks before Eisenhower's arrival from America was therefore welcomed by the majority of the Allied planning staff, who had been working without a designated commander for more than a year and who, for the most part, had no battlefield experience in fighting the Germans. The outgoing 21 Army Group commander, General Paget, had frankly admitted to Churchill that he held out no hope of the invasion succeeding. General Brooke, too, had warned the planners that "it won't succeed"—and most of the planners had come to agree. A predominantly Canadian raid at Dieppe two years before had ended in catastrophe, with thousands of brave Canadians mown down on the Dieppe beach under enemy artillery and machine-gun fire and with neither the Royal Navy nor the RAF able to locate the German coastal batteries, let alone put them out of commission. The result had been slaughter.[4]

Now, however, Montgomery was in sole charge of the ground forces. He had eighteen months' experience of successfully campaigning against the Germans. He had beaten Rommel in the desert again and again, from the defensive battles of Alam Halfa and Medenine to offensive battles such as Alamein and Mareth. He had completely redrafted Husky, the planned Allied invasion of Sicily, and, although there had been a tragic failure in the paratroop drops from friendly fire, the landings themselves had gone like clockwork. They had slowed down thereafter only because of the separation of the two Allied armies and the failure of General Alexander, the ground force commander, to take real control of the land campaign. This time, Monty was adamant, that would not happen. Eisenhower had promised him complete control of the land battle of France—and Monty believed him.

As the chief American planner at COSSAC told the official U.S. historian, "A wave of relief came over us. . . . Monty's action was like a breath of fresh air."[5] In a matter of hours, Gen. Sir Bernard Montgomery (he had been promoted and knighted after the British victory at Alamein) had changed the COSSAC plan for Overlord from one in which almost no one believed to one in which all could put their faith.

Thus, by the time Eisenhower arrived in London two weeks later, after his vacation in the United States, Monty's new plan for Overlord was in place and contested only by General Morgan, the chief staff officer to Overlord's supreme commander, and those senior generals and brigadiers whose noses had been put out of joint by Montgomery's dictatorial takeover. These officers therefore requested a chance to present their case, at their own headquarters in Norfolk House, near Piccadilly, which were to become Eisenhower's also. Once again Monty got up, after their presentation, and tore their Overlord plan apart.

Eisenhower's no-nonsense chief of staff, Walter Bedell-Smith, had welcomed Montgomery's solution to the chaotic planning for Husky the year before (when Monty had outlined it to him on the mirror of the gentleman's toilet at Allied Forces headquarters in Algiers). Once again Lieutenant-General Bedell-Smith primed his boss in advance of the January 21 meeting at Norfolk House. After listening to the two sides, the new supreme commander declared that he backed

Montgomery's plan, as the minutes of the meeting (concealed for forty years) unequivocally reveal: "The Supreme Commander agreed with General MONTGOMERY that it was desirable that the assault should be strengthened and that CHERBOURG"—rather than Caen and the main road to Paris—"should rapidly be captured." Moreover Eisenhower "proposed that General MONTGOMERY should be left in sole charge of the land battle."[6]

The COSSAC refuseniks, still loathe to recast the invasion, went away and formulated their own compromise plan, this time ferrying four, rather than three, divisions onto the narrow Arromanches beachhead—with even greater consequent congestion! Finally, on January 23, 1944, Eisenhower reiterated his decision that Monty's plan be accepted, and informed General Marshall and the Combined Chiefs of Staff in Washington accordingly.

"After detailed examination of the tactical plan," he wrote, "I clearly understand Montgomery's original objection to the narrowness of the assault. Beaches are too few and too restricted to depend upon them as avenues through which all our original build-up would have to flow. We must broaden out to gain quick initial success, secure more beaches for build-up and particularly to get a force at once into the Cherbourg Peninsula behind the natural defensive barrier separating that feature from the mainland. In this way there would be a reasonable hope of gaining the port in short order. We must have this."[7]

It had taken Monty three weeks to get his way, but he could, as before the great Alamein offensive, concentrate now on training and rehearsal of the Allied armies—inspiring the commanders and their staffs, officers, and soldiery to see this as the supreme test of the war: the greatest battle of their lives.

There is not space here to recount in detail the way in which Montgomery prepared his ground forces for the D-Day invasion—but the similarity with the Battle of Alamein remains astonishing. Deception once again was an important tool: Operation Fortitude was designed to fool the Germans into believing the assault would take place in the Pas de Calais.[8] Moreover, as at Alamein, and, later, before the attack on Sicily, all participating formations were made to practice the assault, this time on designated British beaches. Tragedy struck when a flotilla of German motor-torpedo E-boats was permitted by lax British destroyer cover to penetrate one such rehearsal, sinking the landing craft and drowning more than six hundred Americans. But the rehearsals continued.

Meanwhile General Montgomery made it his task to visit and speak in advance to every single formation—American, Canadian, and British—that was to land on D-Day and in the days thereafter. Indeed he was considered such an inspirational speaker that he was asked to go on a tour of British factories to help raise flagging morale in important weapon-producing bottlenecks and to address key railway communications workers. His critics worried lest he become a modern Cromwell in the making. But Montgomery recognized that national morale was vital to the families of the men who would be fighting: relatives whose confidence and pride would help inspire their sons and brothers.

Most importantly, however, Monty wanted the senior commanding and staff officers to be "in the picture" as before Alamein by knowing the larger plan and where they fitted into it.

No other battle of such a scale in human history was planned and rehearsed with such precision and combination of all arms; Montgomery ruthlessly sacked commanders he did not feel were "up to it," all the way down to battalion colonels. Perhaps his greatest feat—the culmination of more than two decades of revolutionary training and modern management in the British army—was the series of conferences he organized with his commanders in January, February, and March culminating thereafter in two great 21 Army Group presentations of plans at his headquarters at St. Paul's School. At these presentations, held in April and May 1944, he went through the master plan and made each army, corps, and divisional commander rehearse openly, on scaled models, their role and command preparations for the invasion—with questions and challenges posed by Monty's 21 Army Group staff. The British role was, he emphasized on April 7, to "protect the eastern flank of First US Army while the latter is capturing Cherbourg," and to "offer a strong front against enemy movement towards the lodgement area from the east," while

"First US Army would break out southwards towards the LOIRE and QUIBERON BAY"—1st U.S. Army then wheeling up to Paris with General Patton's 3rd U.S. Army on its right flank "prepared to cross the river and operate to the N.E." to the Ruhr and Berlin. Hopefully the crossing of the Seine would take place by "D+90," or September 3, 1944.[9]

Even Patton, brought back from disgrace in Sicily and slated to command 3rd U.S. Army later in the campaign, was impressed. No longer did it not "mean a thing" to the cavalryman. This time, he acknowledged, the preparations would help make history—with Berlin their common goal.

Monty was in his element, relishing the greatest role of his life, with some two million soldiers under his ground command. Eisenhower, as supreme commander, backed him "one hundred per cent" in almost all his requests, requirements, and decisions, with one important exception. Before leaving the Mediterranean theater, Churchill had persuaded Eisenhower to back Operation Shingle, in which troops would land ahead of the Allied front line, on the crescent-shaped beach of a small promontory town called Anzio near Rome, to bluff the German divisions currently stalemating General Clark's 5th U.S. Army. A more wasteful, poorly commanded amphibious assault cannot be imagined. With Eisenhower's support ("a brilliant maneuver" for which, Eisenhower's diarist complained, General Alexander would unfortunately "get credit" when it succeeded, since the "long-laid plan" had "developed under Ike"[10]) the Anzio assault was duly launched with Churchill's personal *imprimatur* on January 22, 1944. Unfortunately it proved, in the words of Carlo D'Este, historian of the tragic operation, yet "another Allied near disaster on a scale even larger than Salerno."[11] Instead of bluffing the Germans, Shingle merely demonstrated how easy it was for a ruthless defending army to seal off an enemy landing, thereby forcing the enemy to expend critical air, naval, army, and logistical resources in shoring up the survivors—not to speak of causing unnecessary casualties and bad publicity, which affect public morale.

The complete failure of Shingle to bluff the Germans unfortunately

merely indicated to Churchill and Eisenhower, architects of the assault, that the Allied commanders should be more aggressive in push-
ing inland, not that the scale and strategy of the plan had been wrong
from the start. Thus, convinced that Shingle had failed only through
lack of Allied brio rather than through German opposition, and concerned lest Overlord and the subsequent campaign in Normandy
still prove too difficult an operation of war, both Churchill and
Eisenhower began to press for a secondary landing to aid the main
D-Day effort—an assault landing in the south of France given the
code-name Anvil.

Monty was rendered almost apoplectic by such behind-the-scenes
pressure—aware that Winston Churchill's meddling would make him
as much a liability to his own side as Hitler was to the German armies.
The tragic effects of planning for a major landing in the south of
France, with forces to come under Eisenhower on landing, would be
not only to divide Allied focus on D-Day but also, by requiring landing craft in the Mediterranean, to push the launch of D-Day from
the first week in May 1944 to the following month. To the very end
Anvil would remain, in Montgomery's eyes, a tragic and unnecessary
distraction.

Shingle and Anvil reflected Churchill's continual, irresistible temp-
tation to devise alternative schemes and to meddle in details that
caught his fancy. Thus it was that, shortly before D-Day, he asked to
dine with the Allied ground forces commander of Overlord at the
commander's embarkation headquarters at Portsmouth—and to question the commander's staff.

Churchill had always found it hard to like Montgomery, whom he
once described as "a little man on the make." He even admitted to
sympathy—in one sense, at least—for the Afrika Korps commander
captured after Alamein. "Poor von Thoma," he remarked in Parlia-
ment. "I too, have dined with Montgomery."[12]

Churchill's and Montgomery's conceptions of modern warfare
were poles apart—the one a cavalryman who had charged on horse-
back in the Battle of Omdurman in 1898, the other a professional
infantry officer and battlefield realist. Yet they shared two qualities

that raised them high above their peers: indomitable spirit and a concern for human life.

In Churchill's case, this concern over human casualties made him cringe at the prospect of an all-out battle in northern France, with Hitler able to draw on some sixty German divisions to repel an Allied invasion. Sea power had made Britain, as a tiny offshore island, into a great trading and military empire. Land warfare abroad had never been England's strongest suit—as the loss of its American colonies in 1783 had proved. Thus the winter stalemate in Italy—a campaign he himself had forced his American allies not only to accept but to back with air forces, troops, naval forces, and untold supplies—broke Churchill's heart just as the war on the western front in World War I had once done. If only, using sea power and their aerial navies, the Allies could take advantage of their strengths, not their weaknesses! As in his great Dardanelles disaster in World War I, Churchill did not credit the enemy with superior powers in defense, but blamed the Allied field commanders. The weakness of Shingle was not in its conception, he argued, but in its execution. Had the American General Lucas only struck out boldly from Anzio into the Alban Hills, Churchill and Eisenhower both agreed, the Germans would have had to fall back to their "Gothic" defensive line, north of the Italian capital—saving the Allies countless lives in the struggle for Rome.

Montgomery (who complained that "the whole [Shingle] operation was haphazard and patchy,"[13] and had not been rehearsed in advance), did not agree. Nor did the Germans who yet again proved masterly in their ability to seal off anything but an amphibious assault on the massive scale of Husky, the great Allied invasion of Sicily. Montgomery was as concerned as Churchill with saving men's lives—but after decades of experience in commanding British soldiers, and in fighting such professional opponents as the Germans, he felt Allied dispersion of effort was senseless. The German capacity to react swiftly—drilled and honed in a society dedicated to militarism—was simply too effective to permit the Allies to get away with such gambles, save on the most insignificant pin-prick scale. Moreover, the Russians felt the same.

The Germans *could* be defeated on land, Monty felt, and in solid, all-out battle, where the very size of the forces of air, artillery, and armor, gave the Allied troops the confidence they needed to perform their role doggedly and perseveringly—battle in which the Allies could employ their superior resources to best advantage, acting on a clear master plan, not distracted by alternatives or relying on opportunism. Such a dogged approach required iron nerves, as Montgomery had shown at Alamein. The military writer John Ellis might later label this "brute force,"[14] but if so, it was brute force applied to operations that had a better chance of success than failure, in contrast to the performance of British arms before Alamein, and American forces in Algeria and Tunisia thereafter.

The tension before D-Day was certainly high. The chief American planner at COSSAC later confessed that the staff had had "cold feet" before Montgomery took over[15]—and even in March 1944 Churchill's military secretary, General Ismay, was writing that "a lot of people who ought to know better are taking it for granted that Overlord is going to be a bloodbath on the scale of the Somme and Passchendaele."[16] Field-Marshal Sir Alan Brooke, on the eve of the invasion, noted in his diary, "I am very uneasy about the whole operation. At the best it will fall so very short of the expectation of the bulk of the people, namely all those who know nothing of its difficulties. At the worst it may well be the most ghastly disaster of the whole war."[17]

Because of such concerns, pressure for Anvil had continued for months alongside the preparations for Overlord—in Monty's eyes an infuriating distraction from the main business in hand. While he could not stop Anvil, however, he felt he could stop Churchill from meddling in Overlord—so that when Churchill asked to visit his headquarters and question the 21 Army Group staff directly, Monty asked the prime minister first to come into his office.

There, in the quiet of his study, Montgomery reminded Churchill of his methods of command. "My staff advise me and I give the final decision; they then do what I tell them," he explained—a system of command which had successfully taken a once-defeated 8th Army from Alamein, in Egypt, to the Sangro, in Italy, without a single defeat. Now, in his capacity as the Allied ground force commander for Overlord, Montgomery had two million men under his command. "All over England the troops are beginning to move towards the assembly areas, prior to embarkation," he told the prime minister. It was too late to start changing the plans—indeed if the prime minister began, at this late stage, to criticize their work (Churchill had become almost hysterical over the numbers of clerks and vehicles designated for Normandy) it could only mean one thing: that the prime minister had lost confidence in him as their commander. He could not therefore permit the prime minister to address the staff; he would rather resign.[18]

Winston Churchill, staring into the willful blue-grey eyes of General Montgomery, was infuriated—and humbled. Bearing the overall responsibility for conducting Britain's role in the war against Hitler for four long years, starting in May 1940—eighteen months before the United States entered the war—the prime minister was near to collapsing from anxiety and stress. His need to meddle in Montgomery's domain really signified that he had lost his bearings. Breaking down, the prime minister began to weep.

Once before, in similar circumstances on the beaches of La Panne, near Dunkirk, General Brooke had broken down and wept in front of Montgomery—something which, in a man normally so austere, had moved Montgomery deeply. Pulling out his handkerchief, now, the general got up from behind his desk and tendered it to the prime minister, feeling triumph, but also compassion for the immense political burdens the prime minister carried, knowing how crucial was Churchill's morale for the morale of the whole nation—and its allies.

Eventually the prime minister recovered his composure and promised not to raise the subject when dining with Montgomery's staff next door, where the officers had lined up to meet him. "I'm not allowed to talk to you, gentlemen," Churchill duly announced as he entered the room. "Everyone," Montgomery's first biographer, Alan Moorehead, related, "sensed there had been a crisis. Most of them guessed what had taken place in the study."[19]

In that symbolic interchange, Montgomery had made it clear that—unlike Eisenhower, Alexander, and other senior commanders—

he would brook no interference, and would not allow himself to be blown off course, intimidated, or distracted by the prime minister. As the commander of the Allied armies he, Montgomery, would launch the D-Day invasion as he had planned it. Moreover, although the majority of his staff would stay behind until the beachhead expanded into a secure bridgehead, he would never countenance the prime minister addressing his staff behind his back.

Given the trials ahead, this was just as well.

Thanks to the delay caused by the pressure for Anvil, D-Day was postponed until June 5, 1944; but those who later thought Allied victory was somehow inevitable had little notion of the magnitude of the undertaking, and the number of things that could still go wrong, from bad weather to swift enemy armored reactions.

There was also the sheer greenness of the Allied soldiery. Despite Montgomery's morale-boosting addresses to the men of every brigade that would land on D-Day, the fact remained that most of the troops had never fought in battle before—at least, not against Germans. Among the four Allied army commanders serving under Montgomery, only one general apart from Montgomery had ever commanded an army in battle! Lieutenant-General Dempsey, commanding the British 2nd Army, Lt.-Gen. Harry Crerar, slated to command the Canadian 1st Army once the bridgehead expanded, and Lieutenant-General Bradley, commanding 1st U.S. Army, had each only commanded a corps in battle, in Sicily the previous year. General Patton, who had commanded 7th U.S. Army in Sicily but whose advancement had been frozen after the "slapping incident," would eventually command 3rd U.S. Army in the field—but only once the bridgehead had been built up and the main confrontation with the German armies had taken place.

Contrary to popular belief, however, Montgomery was impressed by George S. Patton. Both were supreme professionals, both were showmen, both insisted on tough training, and both men led from the front. Both found it difficult to suffer fools or yes-men. When Bradley declared that he would use 1st Army to break out from the Cotentin peninsula once it was in Allied hands, Monty therefore demurred. At a meeting of his army commanders on May 29, shortly before the D-Day assault, Monty twice remarked to Bradley that Patton's 3rd U.S. Army, not the 1st U.S. Army, "should take over for the Brittany, and possibly the Rennes operation"—the breakout to the Loire.[20]

Bradley was disappointed, but loyally accepted Montgomery's decision. He had not been impressed by Patton's generalship in Sicily, as Bradley's personal aide noted in his diary: "General Patton, of course, is extremely unpopular in this [1st U.S. Army] headquarters. Most of our officers have carried with them the punctured legend from Sicily."[21] General Bradley, as a very thorough infantry and artillery commander, regarded Patton as a wild, impetuous commander, who demanded too much of his soldiers—indeed, who sometimes veered towards paranoia.

Only the test of battle would now tell—a battle whose plan, on June 4, 1944, was being threatened with postponement owing to the worsening weather in the English Channel. At best this delay would be for only a day or two; at worst for two weeks, when the moon and tides would once again be propitious.

As the ground forces commander, Monty's view was forthright. The original Dieppe raid, in 1942, had been halted initially due to bad weather, allowing German aircraft to spot and bomb some of the landing craft as they assembled in Southampton waters. When the raid was remounted against Monty's advice some weeks later, the troops had encountered German units not only trained to counter a possible attack, but actually conducting a counter-invasion exercise. As a result the raid—which Churchill hoped would impress the Russians—became one of the worst Allied disasters of the war. Overlord must *not* be delayed, Monty felt, as long as the navy could "take us there." The air forces had enjoyed excellent weather while attacking German transportation networks, "and we must accept that it may not be able to do so well on D-Day."[22]

All eyes turned to the supreme commander—for this was a decision only he, as the man responsible for all Allied naval, air, and army operations, could make. To his historic credit, after having caused a whole month's delay because of his vacillation over Anvil, Eisenhower now made the crucial decision, ordering that D-Day be postponed for twenty-four hours. Then, choosing to believe Group Captain Stagg's meteorological forecast, made on June 5, of a looming break in the otherwise forbidding weather pattern, the supreme commander ordered the invasion to proceed. As night fell, the paratroopers of three Allied airborne divisions—82nd U.S. Airborne, 101st U.S. Airborne, and 6th British Airborne—emplaned, while from a host of English south-coast seaports sailed a vast fleet comprising 7 battleships, 2 monitors, 23 cruisers, 3 gunboats, 105 destroyers, and more than 1,000 smaller vessels—with 864 merchant ships and 4,000 landing craft in addition. It was the largest assault armada in human history.

In war, as Montgomery had told George Bernard Shaw (while sitting for Augustus John, who was painting his portrait—which, when completed, Monty so disliked that he refused to pay the artist!), a commander must learn "to make quick decisions, quick decisions. Doesn't matter if you're right or wrong—but you must be able to give quick decisions. As long as fifty-one per cent of your decisions are right, you'll succeed."[23]

That he and his subordinate generals would make many mistakes Monty privately accepted—this was unavoidable in battle, where the enemy had just as much intention of defeating you as you did of defeating him. What Montgomery could ensure, nevertheless, was that his formations landed on the coast of France with such initial strength, mass, breadth, and surprise that, as at Alamein, the ultimate outcome of the battle would be assured—provided the Allies kept their nerve.

Churchill, in his blacker moments, had foreseen the English Channel running in blood, and had warned Eisenhower that, if Overlord failed, they would both "go down together."[24] Eisenhower had therefore clung tenaciously to the notion of a second, later, landing in the south of France—indeed he even prepared a brief, typed communiqué, which he kept in his pocket, announcing to the world that the Normandy landings had failed and the Allies had withdrawn.

For himself Monty refused to believe that the landing could or would fail under his command—his optimism surprising even his closest staff. Having intelligence that the Germans could call on more than a million men in northwestern Europe within three days to repel the invasion and had a 16,000-strong panzer division lurking near the proposed British landings, near Caen, they wondered how he could be so sure of success.

Like the legendary "Blood 'n Guts"—George S. Patton—Bernard Law Montgomery can be seen in some ways as a mad general—indeed this had been his nickname after Dunkirk, when he sought to instill professionalism and courage in his formations in the home forces, at a time when German invasion of Britain seemed not only likely, but likely to succeed. As that threat had receded, he had then begun to prepare, already in 1941 and 1942, for the day when the British army would launch its own cross-Channel invasion to evict the Nazis from France—his determination to lead it so powerful that even his own staff was unsure whether this was war or *opéra bouffe*.

Monty's campaigns in North Africa and the Mediterranean in 1942 and 1943 had shown that he was not engaging in opéra bouffe, that he knew his dark trade better than any other field general in the Allied cause. Yet his very concentration on his destiny, as his country's military savior, made Montgomery at times as otherworldly as his father, Bishop Montgomery, had been. Patton, watching Montgomery directing the D-Day preparations, had noted in his diary that Monty was "an actor, but not a fool"—and Patton was right. The small, wiry Anglo-Irishman, brought up in Tasmania, Australia, had increasingly cast himself in the role of sword-bearer for his nation, to the point where his own family ceased to exist. His motherless son David had been shunted among strangers and schoolmasters and their wives for years; Montgomery shunned his brothers and sisters; he refused to visit his mother or allow her to visit him. In almost every respect his "family" had become his men: from his handpicked personal staff to his headquarters staff and, beyond them, the officers and "soldiery."

Monty's drilling, steel grey-blue eyes missed nothing on inspections. He had himself commanded every unit and formation from platoon to army group—and what he looked for in his soldiers was clarity, energy, intelligence, application, loyalty, and courage. His mobile Tactical Headquarters for Normandy had already been set up in advance, outside his headquarters near Portsmouth, with tents, caravans, and trucks, while movement and radio signal communications were rehearsed *in advance*. He neither smoked nor drank. He went to bed early and rose at dawn. Since Alamein he had adopted the simplest of clothes on the battlefield—a tie-less shirt or turtle-neck sweater and baggy corduroy pants, with just a black beret bearing his two distinctive badges, so that he would be instantly recognized by his troops. He liked simple food and enjoyed the company of young officers whom he could tease, train, and help to advance in their careers. Out of that familial bond, moreover, he had, since his takeover in the desert, begun to operate a unique system of personal links with his subordinate commanders: his liaison officers.

Numbering over forty British, American, Canadian, and French officers by the end of the campaign, the system was designed so that, as army group commander, Monty could obtain, every evening, an accurate personal report on and from his subordinates that detailed their positions, their strengths, their plans, their morale. From these reports he could decide whom to visit the following day, whom to encourage in difficulty, whom to congratulate, whom to chide—and whom to dismiss. Had the system been operated by any other commander, the young officers—captains and majors in their twenties—would have been resented and even rejected by subordinate commanders. Under Monty's charge, however, they were seen as what they were: the commander in chief's "eyes and ears," akin to Lord Wellington's "gallopers." Not only would they prove their worth in Normandy, they would help save the Allied armies in the Battle of the Bulge.

General Bradley was awed by the manner in which Montgomery had thought out everything in advance and the extent to which he had shaped the coming battle to ensure that the 1st U.S. Army would achieve its primary object, the capture of Cherbourg—even to the point of switching the planned airdrop of 82nd U.S. Airborne Division from Caen, on the eve of D-Day, to the Carentin estuary. Himself a shy, unassuming officer, Bradley was also amazed at the way

Monty won the hearts of ordinary soldiers. "Psychologically the choice of Montgomery as British Commander for the OVERLORD assaults came as a stimulant to us all," Bradley later wrote. "For the thin, ascetic face that stared from an unmilitary turtle-neck sweater had, in little over a year, become a symbol of victory in the eyes of the Allied world. . . . But nowhere did the slight, erect figure of Montgomery in his baggy and unpressed corduroys excite greater assurance than among the soldiers themselves. Even Eisenhower with all his engaging ease could never stir American troops to the rapture with which Monty was welcomed by his men. Among those men the legend of Montgomery had become an imperishable fact."[25]

At gatherings of between three thousand and six thousand men, standing on the hood of his American jeep and wearing his trademark black beret, Monty had, with the aid of a microphone, addressed every soldier bound for France—telling them the importance of their mission—that the future of the free world rested on their courage—and assuring them they would be "reverently buried" if they fell in battle. . . .

As he had before Alamein, Monty also addressed every senior officer in 21 Army Group, reviewing the plan of battle. This was modern leadership for a modern democracy, making the distant generalship of World War I a thing of the past. The prayers of many millions went with him and his troops as they embarked—and no participant would ever forget the sight that greeted the eyes when dawn broke on June 6, 1944: almost six thousand vessels making for the shores of Normandy in the greatest amphibious assault landing in the annals of warfare.

D-Day

T HE TRIUMPH of the D-Day landings was that Montgomery's plan exerted such overwhelming power over such a wide (sixty-mile) front that, even though specific assaults faltered (as at Omaha Beach), the landings as a group swept all opposition before them. Thus, although the Germans managed to hold back until late afternoon the left flank of the first American troops to land, and although 21 Panzer Division, with sixteen thousand panzer grenadiers, counterattacked and wedged itself for some hours between the British and Canadian assaults, the American landings on Utah beach were a walkover, while the Anglo-Canadian landings on Sword, Juno, and Gold smashed their way ashore and were well inland by nightfall. Eisenhower would not need his piece of paper.

The Allied air forces had done their job thoroughly, and the power of naval guns had provided the same sort of heavy artillery support that the advancing infantry of Highlanders, South Africans, New Zealanders, and Australians had enjoyed on the first night of the Battle of Alamein, so that hardly any seacraft had been lost to Luftwaffe attack. The Allied navies had in fact performed magnificently, landing some 129,000 soldiers by nightfall on the first day. A further 26,000 British and American paratroopers had dropped from the air or had landed in gliders. Although the most optimistic scenario—the seizure of both Caen and Bayeux on D-Day itself—was not achieved, all targeted beaches were in Allied hands, and the eastern flank along the river Orne had been secured in some of the most miraculously successful paratroop landings in history (for example, on Pegasus Bridge). The Allies had only to link their four beachheads into a single, contiguous sixty-mile front before moving on to part two of Montgomery's plan, in which the Americans would capture Cherbourg and the Cotentin peninsula from the inferior infantry of the German Seventh Army, and the British and Canadians would simultaneously attack Caen and lock horns with the main infantry and panzer divisions of Panzer Group West and the German Fifteenth Army.

Military historians would later cavil at the Allied failures—particularly the failure of British and Canadian forces to take Caen in the first few hours or days, and secure sites for airfields to the south of the city. However, Monty, who landed by destroyer early on the morning of June 8, was unperturbed. He had willingly changed orders for the crucial airborne division that would have guaranteed Caen's immediate capture so that he could ensure the success of the U.S. right flank at Carentan—the gateway to Cherbourg. Like a master chess player, he knew it would be a long battle and that, with a million troops to call upon, the Germans would not give in any more easily than they had at Alamein. Only by maintaining a mortal threat to Paris and the Pas de Calais could he bring the main German forces to battle and destroy their ability to resist. As he did so, he would relentlessly build up his own bridgehead (as at Alamein) so that, at the appropriate moment, he could break out with armor in an area where the enemy's resistance had been broken. In Normandy, this meant threatening the main route to Paris, from Caen, while expanding behind it in the Cherbourg peninsula a vast arsenal of troops and weapons too powerful for the Germans to hold back and which would provide a launch point for Allied forces to eventually smash their way out to Brittany and the Loire. Ten thousand casualties had been suffered in the initial Allied assault, but the Allies were now firmly established on the mainland of France and backed by massive naval artillery and immense air power. Only a single German panzer division had managed to see action on day one, and its tanks had been swiftly driven back, lest they become cut off. The slogging match could now begin.

Within four days Montgomery's armies joined all their beachheads and threw out a continuous line from the River Orne in the east almost to Caumont in the center, and halfway across the Cotentin peninsula in the west. It was a brilliant achievement. Before the end of the month, while 2nd Army drew upon itself the bulk of the primary German armored and infantry divisions in the west, Bradley's 1st U.S. Army was able to seal off the entire Cherbourg peninsula—and the third great phase of the Battle of Normandy could begin.

July 1944 would, however, be a cruel month for the Allies, seeing week after week of bitter hedgerow fighting, both around the city of Caen and in the *bocage* around St. Lo. Moreover, there would be more storms in the English Channel—and in the Allied rear headquarters.

Behind the scenes—at Supreme Allied Headquarters in England; in the War Office in London; at Royal Air Force (RAF) Bomber Command; at U.S. Army Air Force (USAAF) Command; and at other remote headquarters—the sheer tension of watching the battle for France, indeed for Europe, unfold a mere hundred miles away across the Channel often proved too much for certain senior officers.

Montgomery, as sole ground force commander, might be perfectly happy with the way the battle was progressing, despite the Germans' fierce counterattacks and their brilliant defense of Caen. General Bradley might be equally satisfied with the performance of his largely "unblooded" American army in the unfamiliar Normandy terrain, as was General Dempsey with his Anglo-Canadian army. Those officers left behind in England, however, chafed at the passage of time and the perceived slowness of Allied gains with which to mark up their maps. This was unjust, but psychologically understandable.

The tension was worst for General Eisenhower, however, because he was the interface between the Combined Chiefs of Staff and the field commander of Overlord, as well as between naval and air commanders in England and Montgomery in France. It was his responsibility to send daily progress reports on the battle—on which the eyes of the world were fixed—to London and Washington. Great matters were at stake. The Soviets, engaged in desperate fighting with the German divisions on the eastern front, had waited two years for a promised second front that would draw off German divisions, especially panzer divisions, to the west. A swift victory in Normandy would lead, inevitably, to the collapse of the Third Reich; Allied deadlock, even defeat, would allow Hitler to redouble German efforts in the east.

Montgomery, exercising his command from his tactical headquarters only two miles from the front in Normandy, was well aware of such expectations and anxieties, but counseled patience. The Battle of Alamein had lasted only twelve days, but in that time defeatist tongues had bruited stories of stalemate and failure leading even the prime minister, at one moment, to lose heart. The Battle of Normandy would take longer, and incite even more tongue-wagging and back-seat driving, Montgomery knew—yet he was supremely confident that as long as the Allied armies fought the Germans according to his overall strategy, he would beat Rommel in a prolonged "ding-dong" battle, at the furthest extremity of the Germans' lines of communication, as at Alamein. Hitler would never allow von Runstedt or Rommel to pull back to a better defensive line—Normandy would thus be, both sides knew, the deciding battle of World War II in the west. Allied victory would come in time, Montgomery was certain, so long as his armies committed no major tactical blunders and held steadfastly to his overall strategy: engaging Rommel's armored and infantry forces offensively on the British and Canadian left flank, while persistently expanding the American bridgehead in the Cherbourg peninsula behind.

On the eve of D-Day, Winston Churchill had told his wife that twenty thousand men might be dead by the time she awoke; he had told Eisenhower that the Overlord armies would be doing magnificently well if they reached Paris by the first snows in December. Yet somehow the fact that D-Day casualties had been far below expectations and the initial assault so spectacularly successful caused Churchill to forget this timetable. At both of his great presentations at St. Paul's School, Montgomery had warned of the "dog-fight" that would ensue, as at Alamein, after the break-in—yet within days Churchill himself began to criticize Monty for slowness. In an unpublished manuscript, Eisenhower later recalled how Churchill was so "especially disappointed by the failure on our left to capture Caen" that the prime minister even made a personal visit to Eisenhower, bypassing the Combined Chiefs of Staff. "He pointed out that at the final pre-invasion briefing [at St. Paul's school] the seizure of Caen within 24 hours had been assumed. Our failure, after many days of fighting to seize this key city, strengthened his fear that we were descending into a bitter 'trench-warfare' situation similar to that of World War I or, at best, were experiencing on a larger scale the early results of Anzio."[1]

Such carping reminded Montgomery of Alamein, all over again.

War is an option of difficulties, Gen. James Wolfe once remarked. Under National Socialism the German armed forces had, after 1933, created a veritable über-class of outstanding reserve officers and senior commanders backed by obedient, well-armed, and resourceful troops. The Allies not only had started later, but simply were not in the same militaristic league—and their defeats, from Dunkirk to Luzon, showed the disparity.

Montgomery's genius was to recognize that, in a modern democracy, the largely civilian soldiery—whether volunteer or conscripted—made poor killers unless their backs were to the wall—and in France not even the wall had been enough to make Frenchmen fight hard, let alone offer up their lives. Monty realized that as military leaders in a modern democracy the Allied leaders had to do more than simply inspire their men with a cause; they also needed to recognize their obligation to train their men to fight the Germans successfully, and they needed to feel a genuine accountability for their men's lives—an accountability so brutally, criminally absent in World War I.

This was by no means a simple task. Neither the small interwar British army nor the still smaller interwar U.S. army had been able to expand overnight into armored, infantry, and artillery forces capable of the sort of interarms professional cooperation that German soldiers seemed almost by nature to evince. Worse still, despite tremendous and ever-growing air power, and despite the fact that the American air forces were still nominally part of the U.S. army, true interservice cooperation was not taught or practiced by the Allied air or ground forces; it simply evolved in response to the necessities of battle against an enemy as stubborn, obedient, and willing to die as the Germans.

In the British forces this failure on the part of soldiers to work with other arms as part of a larger military team was compounded by the British class system, which spilled over as a sort of caste-snobbery within and between the three services. The Royal Navy considered itself the "senior service," while the RAF, having claimed its military liberation from the army in 1918, considered itself involved in an almost wholly independent fight against the Third Reich. Such attitudes were reflected even in distinctive British uniforms—especially those for women—that emphasized the three different services, and presented an interesting contrast with the more monochromatic colors of German service apparel. Within the British army, moreover, the old habits of empire died hard: relying on others to do the "donkey" work. In World War I on the western front, the poet Robert Graves had noted that when British battalions that had been stationed in India went into the line the men still bore the arrogance, complacency, stupidity, and closed minds of imperialists. "The men treat the French civilians just like 'niggers,' kick them about, talk army Hindustani at them."[2] Only the bitter reality of fighting German foes could teach such men they would die unless they learned new behavior. The success of Hitler's Third Reich and Hirohito's Japan had once again taught British soldiers to respect German and Japanese military forces in the field, but not how to match them successfully in modern combat. Using his legendary skills as a trainer as well as a leader Montgomery had recast his 8th Army into a legendary fighting force against the Germans in North Africa. Then, with new formations in 8th Army, he had done the same in Sicily and Italy. Now, however, he commanded two million soldiers from all nations participating in the Battle of Normandy—the majority of whom were inexperienced in battle.

Monty's historic task, therefore, was not only to promote a ruthlessly professional approach to planning and training for modern battle, but to inspire his officers and men to fight in Normandy—not simply to get ashore, but to go on fighting all-out for three months of unrelenting battle thereafter and if necessary, to die doing so. After the obscene and pointless casualties of World War I on the western front, "for king and country" had become an inadequate motivation for self-sacrifice. Modern battle, however—especially battle against the Nazis—required modern approaches to command. Driving every single day to inspect, decorate, and be seen by his troops was for Montgomery an essential feature of democratic generalship.

By dint of extraordinary leadership Montgomery had provided this inspiration in the run-up to D-Day, and he continued to do so in the battle that followed—a battle that became the greatest test of applied Allied offensive warfare in World War II. For the first time since their operations in Sicily the Allied airborne divisions played a significant role in battle. Tactical cooperation between the army and the air force on the battlefield improved beyond recognition; the air forces, given flyable weather, attacked anything German that moved on the ground; and the navy not only ferried—across the English Channel and across the Atlantic, direct from Canada and America—the vast arsenals of weaponry and stores needed for the struggle in France, but off the coast of France it continued to provide supporting naval firepower that took out German land targets for more than six weeks after the first men touched down.

For this cohesion of interservice effort—a truly "combined operation"—General Eisenhower, as supreme allied commander, would be justly accorded high praise, both then and later. For Montgomery, as architect, trainer, and single ground force commander of the

D-Day Allied invasion armies, the praise was unstinting in the days after news of the successful invasion—but, as the campaign in Normandy reached its "dog-fight" stage, the plaudits became more and more muted.

As Bradley noted, the British and Canadian role on the eastern flank of the bridgehead was self-sacrificing, since there was no possibility of breaking out there, given the amount of German armor and high-quality infantry blocking direct access to the Pas de Calais and Paris. As Bradley wrote later, Montgomery "did not ever envision a major 'breakout' from his lodgement; the major breakout was to be conducted by my forces. . . . Monty would absorb the main shock of the enemy counterattack, pin down as many of the enemy as possible (keeping them off my forces), providing the solid nub on which we could turn our wheel."[3] Thus it is understandable why the infantry and armored troops who fought around the "nub" of Caen were disheartened when Cherbourg fell on June 26, with 30,000 Germans surrendering to U.S. Lt. Gen. "Lightning Joe Collins," but the Germans held onto Caen itself, in spite of the 2nd Army's repeated efforts to encircle it, until finally the southern suburbs were captured on July 8, 1944—four long and bloody weeks after D-Day.

Napoleon had noted that morale is to matériel as three is to one—and it is to Montgomery's credit that his visits to his front line commanders at their forward headquarters and his visibility on the field kept faith in the outcome of the battle high. Yet the fighting itself in the Anglo-Canadian sector was as savage as that on the western front in World War I had been. By the end of June 1944 British and Canadian units had already suffered 25,000 casualties—without the capture of a German-held city to tout on the eastern flank, beyond Bayeux. Moreover, on the American western flank, post-Cherbourg operations—delayed by terrible late June storms that wrecked the American floating Mulberry harbor and set back the American timetable of attack—became grindingly slow in the difficult *bocage* countryside near St. Lo. The possibility of deadlock such as occurred in World War I was a real cause for fear, and Montgomery became so concerned about the potentially infectious nature of this fear that he even banned the general distribution of after-action reports. Many

British battalions lost every fighting company commander, and the possibility of a shortage of replacements became a growing anxiety at the War Office.

A major cause of discontent in the Allied rear-camp was the lack of good airfields within the bridgehead. By pulling two panzer divisions from the Russian front, Hitler and his generals were able to stem General Dempsey's second outflanking move to envelop Caen from the west, but although this accorded with Montgomery's tactics (similar to those he employed at Alamein) of drawing the enemy armor into a battle of attrition while his other armor-backed infantry worked their way south, the slowness of the British and Canadians to capture Caen and make room for more airfields out of German artillery range disappointed some air barons, who forgot the overall tactical military strategy Montgomery had so clearly outlined at St. Paul's School—and who, feeling that they had been "promised" airfields by a certain date, now spread fears of stalemate, calling for Monty's replacement.

Ironically, the air commander of Overlord, Air Marshal Leigh-Mallory, was perfectly satisfied by the airfield situation, because the short distance from his south-of-England airfields made it logistically easier for RAF and USAAF squadrons to be serviced and in no way impeded their ability to support the ground forces. Unfortunately Leigh-Mallory—though a hero of the Battle of Britain—was out of his depth in arguing with men like Deputy Supreme Commander Air Marshal Tedder or General Spaatz, the head of the USAAF forces, or even Air Vice Marshal Coningham, the Tactical Air Force chief whose jealousy of Montgomery and intrigue grew to malevolence of a Shakespearean scale in July.

Who would such barons have preferred as ground force commander? There was talk of General Alexander being summoned from Italy—but Alexander's performance in "masterminding" Salerno, Anzio, and Monte Cassino gave no reason to believe he would ever have got two Allied armies successfully ashore, let alone have been able to direct the armies of a swelling bridgehead in Normandy that the Germans were unable to rope off.

In the same way, those—including President Roosevelt, General Marshall, Air Marshal Tedder, and Coningham—who urged Eisenhower to take over field command of the Allied armies himself, were simply ignoring the fact that, as supreme commander, Eisenhower was already filling a crucial need in his interservice "political" role and had no field experience of commanding formations in battle—indeed had no field headquarters ready from which to exercise such field command! When he did establish one in mid-August, it was at Granville, on the Atlantic coast of the Cotentin peninsula. "Why SHAEF [Supreme Headquarters, Allied Expeditionary Force] picked this remote spot," American historian Carlo D'Este wondered, "is one of the great mysteries of the war: not only was Granville remote and inaccessible, but it lacked adequate communications," and communications capacity is the cardinal necessity for a modern tactical headquarters.[4] Nor had Eisenhower ever come up with any tactical battle plan of his own in the entire war, other than the completely unnecessary bombing and seizure of the island of Pantelleria in the early summer of 1943! Moreover, such ideas as Eisenhower did hold with regard to tactical approaches to fighting the Germans were, in Montgomery's eyes, the same as those of the "butchers" of World War I: attack everywhere, all of the time. Eisenhower, Marshall, Bradley, and other American career infantrymen schooled at Fort Leavenworth were wedded to "the unyielding principle of applying constant pressure across an entire front," as the American military historian Carlo D'Este explained[5]—an approach that assumed the enemy would thereby crack or run away, or both.

Montgomery's experience fighting the Germans had taught him that the Germans didn't simply crack or run away—at least, not unless they were first stretched in anticipation of an attack, then dealt an overwhelmingly powerful, sudden blow in a strategically chosen place: the Schwerpunkt. At Alamein, Montgomery had proved in battle that such tactics worked when Rommel proved unable to hold back the massive penetration Montgomery's forces made in the northern sector of his line, and which Montgomery kept reinforcing until, while the Germans were held in "do or die" combat on the Alamein coast road, he was able to punch a hole through their weaker defenses further inland. In France, he was now fighting a similar battle, but on a scale ten times bigger.

In these circumstances, with the battle's two primary leaders, with different conceptions of warfare, operating from two locations— Montgomery at the front in France and Eisenhower at the rear in England—and with Eisenhower's Allied rear headquarters, more-over, split into a jumbled web of different locations in southern Britain, owing to the launching of Hitler's "secret weapon," the pi-lotless V1 bomber, on June 13—the greatest of all Allied battles might well have come to grief in the summer of 1944 after a bril-liant beginning.

Fortunately, this didn't happen—and it is instructive to ex-amine why.

Montgomery admired Patton's ability to seize and retain the initiative, but was anxious not to use Patton's great powers of armored leader-ship until Rommel's primary forces had been attacked and worn down on the coastal flank.[6] Even on the western flank American tanks could easily be picked off by concealed 88s and anti-tank weapons con-cealed in the bocage, where double tree-lined boundaries, separated by a ditch, bordered every field. Thus, although Patton's 3rd U.S. Army headquarters was set up in Normandy in the first week of July 1944, Monty ordered that it not be activated until St. Lo was taken and Bradley's American forces had first broken the German cordon to the west, at Avranches.

Careless though he might be of the travails of his countrymen around St. Lo (where American forces had a 3–1 superiority in in-fantry and 8–1 superiority in tank numbers), Patton was neverthe-less excited by the prospects that Montgomery, as the ground force commander, held out to him. After lunching with Montgomery at 21 Army Group headquarters in the Cerisy Forest at Blay on July 7, 1944, Patton recorded in his diary, "Montgomery went to great length explaining why the British had done nothing" around Caen. Once the 1st U.S. Army reached Avranches, however, Patton's role, Mont-gomery had explained, would be to leave three divisions at Avranches and peel off his ten remaining divisions on the Loire flank of the 1st

Army, directing them in an end-run, striking straight for Paris and forcing the main body of German troops that were struggling to hold back Dempsey and Bradley's armies to retreat. "When I do start, I will, if current plans hold, have a swell chance," Patton wrote to his wife the next day.[7]

Bradley's first attempt to get to Avranches, however, foundered south of St. Lo, just as Dempsey's repeated attempts to envelop Caen had been unsuccessful. For a moment, on July 10, Bradley confessed that he seemed to have failed. It was at this juncture, with Dempsey offering to try to mount an alternative breakout towards Falaise on the eastern flank, that Monty showed his caliber as a great field commander. As Dempsey related to the American official historian, "Monty quietly replied: 'Never mind. Take all the time you need, Brad.' Then he went on to say: 'If I were you I think I should concentrate my forces a little more'—putting two fingers together on the map in his characteristic way. Then he turned to me and said: 'Go on hitting: drawing the German strength, especially some of the armour, onto yourself—so as to ease the way for Brad.'"[8]

Sadly, such patient planning at the front, in Normandy, would become subsumed by later historiography, as "national"—or nationalistic—historians and filmmakers sought to rewrite the great Battle of Normandy as a stalled British operation, rescued by American opportunism in breaking out of the *bocage*.

The unfolding of Montgomery's overall strategy, it has to be admitted, had certainly been beset by problems, as the Germans fought for every yard of Norman soil—knowing it was, ultimately, the decisive battle of the west. As Monty explained, in a hand-delivered letter to Field-Marshal Brooke on July 14, the 1st U.S. Army had been "battling its way since 3 July through very difficult country, thickly wooded and very marshy, and with canalized avenues of approach to enemy positions. The Americans have had had very heavy casualties; but they have stuck it well." Once the 1st U.S. Army won "a footing on the road PERIERS ST. LO, it will be able to launch a real 'blitz' attack with fresh troops," he confided his plan to Brooke. "This attack would break in on a narrow front with great air support, and fresh divisions would pass through the gap. I have discussed the problem with Bradley and this operation will be launched on 19 or 20 July."[9] The operation was given the code-name Cobra.

To mask this concentrated American assault, and to ensure the Germans did not release panzer reserves from the British eastern sector to block it, Monty had, he also revealed to Brooke, ordered Dempsey to mount a feint southwest of Caen, on the day before Cobra, to kick off on July 18: Operation Goodwood. With the Germans struggling to hold back Dempsey's attack—similar to the Australian infantry attack to the north of Alamein—Bradley would finally be in a position to break out on the other flank of the bridgehead, as the New Zealanders had done in Operation Supercharge at Alamein.

Goodwood, its path paved by a massive air attack by British heavy bombers, duly went ahead as promised on July 18, 1944. The planned breakout by General Bradley's forces, Operation Cobra, unfortunately did not. Instead, the offensive was postponed, owing to bad weather that made impossible the heavy American "carpet" bombing that was integral to the plan. Each day's postponement deepened the anxiety of people at home.

Montgomery was unfazed by the delay. After all, his "Supercharge" attack at Alamein had similarly been delayed while General Freyberg— the New Zealand commander he had picked to lead the breakout— assembled his forces. In rear headquarters in England, however, there was once again consternation—for General Dempsey, anxious not to suffer too many casualties in what was a feint attack, closed down his Goodwood attack after only thirty-six hours. His tanks and infantry had by then cleared the last Germans from Caen and extended the British line by about seven miles, but had completely failed to reach their supposed objective, Falaise—the Germans having shown their legendary anti-tank gunnery skills with 88s, Tigers, and even Panther tanks that stopped the British armored advance cold, indeed forced the British to withdraw from the Bourguébus Ridge they had reached at the cost of 400 tanks and 5,500 casualties.

Had Bradley's identical attack, preceded by American heavy bombers, been launched the next day as originally intended, the air barons and other subversives would have had the wind taken from their sails, since Monty could have shown the two linked operations—a punch to the enemy's solar plexus, with an immediate right hook to knock him over—taking place on the map of Normandy. But with Bradley forced to delay his American kick-off seemingly indefinitely, it looked once again as if Montgomery had failed to worst the Germans and the campaign was bogging down.

Thus, unaware that the German commanders were in desperation counseling Hitler to allow them to retreat, Eisenhower found himself besieged at his headquarters by suggestions and recommendations for avoiding what looked like an approaching stalemate. Chief among these recommendations was the resurrection of Anvil, the proposed Allied landing on the Mediterranean coast of France, near Marseilles, which had delayed the Normandy campaign by a month. There were, however, many others—such as landing Patton's 3rd U.S. Army divisions in a surprise attack on the coast of Brittany.

In America, there was increasing pressure for Eisenhower to use the vast strategic (heavy) bomber forces to pulverize "the Germans"— without the least notion what this meant, and regardless of the fact that the heavy bomber pilots and bombardiers had never been ordered by their commanding officers to train for a close-support role! Fifty years before the development of "smart bombs," such notions amounted to fantasies not only because they took no account of the inaccuracy of high-altitude bombing, but also because they ignored the war going on between the air barons themselves. Thus the commander of the Overlord air forces, Air Marshal Leigh-Mallory, remained determined to help Montgomery in any way he could— threatening "to resign" unless he was given "the whole Air Forces available to the full and immediate support of the Army," and the "policy of double-dealing" or backstabbing was stopped.[10] The deputy supreme commander, Air Marshal Tedder, and Leigh-Mallory's own subordinate, Air Marshal Coningham, remained determined, by contrast, to unseat Montgomery—and get rid of Leigh-Mallory for pressing for the heavy air forces to be used in direct support of the armies!

It was small wonder, then, that Eisenhower was torn in multiple directions, as the chorus of anti-Montgomery voices at the various rear headquarters of SHAEF grew to a crescendo. On the night of July 19, for example, Tedder had telephoned Eisenhower, his boss, "and said that the British chiefs of staff would support any recommendation that Ike might care to make," Eisenhower's diarist noted, "meaning that if Ike wanted to sack Monty for not succeeding in going places with his big three armored division push, he would have no trouble, officially."[11]

Aware of Tedder's machinations, Field-Marshal Brooke immediately flew to Monty's headquarters in Normandy to order him to abandon his "no visitors" policy and invite both Eisenhower and the Churchill to his tactical headquarters. Monty was, he made clear, to give them each a renewed personal presentation of his tactical master plan—knowing that they would be awed by Monty's absolute clarity and control of the battlefield.

Brooke was right. Eisenhower, emerging from Monty's map truck on July 20, seemed a changed man. He'd been suffering listlessness and ringing in his ears. Now, after hearing Monty's report—in which he pointed out that, thanks to the British and Canadians locking some four German corps in close combat around Caen, Bradley would have some 750 American tanks facing at most 100 panzers once the delayed Cobra operation got underway—Eisenhower asked to go fishing, piloted his own plane, and told his diarist to call his chief of staff, Bedell Smith, and "caution him against even hinting at the subject we have been discussing": the sacking of Montgomery.[12]

Churchill, likewise, emerged from Monty's tented headquarters a rejuvenated man the next day, July 21—especially since he had heard the latest news: that German officers had mounted a putsch against Hitler, planting a bomb at the Führer's Rastenburg headquarters in East Prussia. For Churchill, as prime minister, this secret information—gleaned from Ultra—promised to alter the entire political situation, since the generals behind the putsch would, if it proved successful, undoubtedly sue for peace.

Frustratingly, the putsch against Hitler came to grief when the Führer emerged shaken but alive from the smoking ruins of his forest headquarters, the "Wolf's Lair." Moreover, on the battlefield Monty's plans once more were thrown off when bad weather yet again delayed Bradley's kick-off, from July 20 to July 24. Tragically, some of the American heavy bombers were recalled too late—not only failing to abort their mission, but bombing by mistake their own American troops, including a senior American general visiting from the United States. In rear headquarters in England, this was seen as a yet another bad omen for the Allies.

Mercifully on July 25, 1944, seven long days after the intended kick-off date of Operation Cobra, the weather turned favorable. Fifteen hundred aircraft from 9th U.S. Air Force flew south across Normandy and dropped 3,400 tons of bombs to clear a way through the German front lines—a sort of air version of a World War I artillery "creeping barrage." Once again a number of stray bombs hit American troops, killing more than a hundred and wounding many more. Eisenhower, who had had to approve the order for heavy bombers to fulfill this new army-support role (instead of attacking strategic installations well behind the enemy lines) was furious, and wanted to call off any further such attacks. "I gave them the green light on this show but this is the last one" he stated.[13] At the battlefront, however, General Collins found the enemy stunned, indeed almost obliterated, and ordered his men to keep going. On July 27, Bradley then put in his American armor.

It was, finally, akin to the last days of Alamein—the rear-headquarter commanders and staffs losing heart at the very moment when the front-line armor began to break out. For, despite the interval between Goodwood and Cobra, the Germans had kept the vast majority of their armor and artillery on Dempsey's flank for too long, and with Allied aircraft controlling the skies it was now too late for them to stop Bradley's narrow-fronted American assault from breaking through their girdle. Rommel—the last senior German commander left from D-Day—had been so convinced the British were going to "launch the thrust against PARIS," followed by a "large scale landing" in the Pas de Calais, as he reported in mid-July after the fall of Caen,[14] that he had overlooked the possibility of a primary breakout in the American sector, to the south—and had remained convinced Patton was still in England, preparing to mount a second cross-Channel attack near Calais!

The success of Cobra, and the exhilarating days in late July and early August when the German armies fell apart, were to Montgomery the vindication of the tactical strategy he had employed since D-Day. For Eisenhower, who had confirmed Monty's continuing role as single ground commander of the Allied armies in Normandy, it raised, however, the question of who would take field command of the two Allied army groups, once Patton's 3rd U.S. Army became operational, General Hodges took over command of the 1st U.S. Army, General Simpson took command of the 9th U.S. Army, and General Bradley was promoted to become 12th American Army Group commander, alongside Montgomery's 21 Army Group.

On the German side, almost all the senior German generals had by now been dismissed, wounded, or killed—or had killed themselves in despair. General Dollmann, the commander of the 7th Army facing the Normandy beachhead, had committed suicide on June 28 as British forces crossed the Odon, west of Caen; General von Schweppenburg, commander of Panzer Group West, had been dismissed by Hitler for pleading to be allowed to withdraw to the Seine on July 6 (the very day when Churchill complained about Monty's slowness in seizing Caen, leading Field-Marshal Brooke to "flare up" and ask "if he could not trust his generals for five minutes instead of continuously abusing them and belittling them"[15]), while General von Rundstedt, commander in chief in the west, had also been sacked by Hitler on July 2 for calling the battle lost and allegedly telling him to "make peace, you fool!" And when Rommel, as commander in chief of Army Group B, was severely wounded by an Allied fighter attack on July 17 in the aptly named hamlet Ste. Foy de Montgomery, von Rundstedt's successor, General von Kluge—a specialist in dealing with armored breakthroughs on the Russian front—found himself forced to take over Rommel's field command as well as continuing his job as supreme German commander in the west, lest the German armies collapse.

General Eisenhower was in the reverse situation—witnessing the triumphant culmination of Montgomery's battle in Normandy. However, the political pressures on him to assume field command in France, as well as directing SHAEF, were becoming more and more urgent, given the growing preponderance of American arms and men. The expectation at SHAEF had always been that Eisenhower would one day move his headquarters to France and take over as ground force commander in chief. In Marshall's eyes, especially, it was high time General Eisenhower left his bunker in England and got "stuck in" as the senior American commander in Europe.

For Eisenhower, however, it was not so simple. He had, it was true, made a British airman his deputy supreme commander for Overlord (in contrast to his choice in the Mediterranean theater), allowing him to be able to deal directly with his army commanders and thereby learn "the ropes." Yet since D-Day Eisenhower had only found time to visit Montgomery, his ground force commander, four times, and his army commanders on the eastern flank even fewer times! He had not established an effective tactical command headquarters in France, and still had no experience of giving battlefield orders, however used he was to exercising rear-headquarter oversight and authority. Nor did he feel he had, as yet, an American field commander whom he could trust to be his deputy, if he asked Air Marshal Tedder to vacate the job. In Normandy, General Bradley had only been fighting in command of an American army for a few weeks—and then under Montgomery's command (Bradley still called Monty "sir"). There was thus no serious possibility Eisenhower could have elevated Bradley to become his deputy supreme commander and Allied ground force commander in battlefield control of five Allied armies—even if the Combined Chiefs of Staff approved such a decision, which was unlikely.

In such circumstances, Eisenhower did the only thing possible: he put off the moment when he would himself take charge in the field and confirmed that General Montgomery would temporarily retain tactical command of the Allied armies in Normandy until the Allies reached the Seine.

General Montgomery was delighted—not simply out of vanity, but because, as a professional soldier through and through, he abhorred passivity as nature abhors a vacuum—naturally more so with the campaign building to its crescendo. However, Eisenhower's decision merely deferred the problem of Allied field command to a later date.

In the meantime, though, the great Battle of Normandy came to a climax. Following Collins's success in Cobra, Patton's 3rd U.S. Army burst from the American dam at Avranches, at the base of the Cherbourg Peninsula—and the Germans, forbidden to retreat by the Führer himself, put up a last, Custer-like stand, on an east-west line in Normandy, running to the south of Caen, Evrecy, and Caumont. Hitler was not only behaving exactly as Montgomery had expected, but he also was taking the risk of his forces becoming en-trapped—just as he had done with his orders to stand fast at Alamein, as the British armor swept around the Axis flank, in November 1942.

Whatever was said about him in England, Montgomery had held to his overall strategy from the beginning: holding the Germans on his Caen flank, while patiently expanding behind it until he could wheel fresh forces through the Cherbourg peninsula to the Loire and then the Seine—cutting off and liberating Brittany, to the west, at the very moment that his breakout armor swung eastward to Paris.

To read Montgomery's war diary, letters, memoranda, and orders to his commanders during the three-month Battle of Normandy, as well as the interviews given after the war by his subordinates, is to marvel at Monty's absolute self-confidence and certainty that, if the Allies simply held firm to this strategy, he would win for them the decisive battle of 1944—just as, at Alamein, he had won the decisive battle of 1942. Moreover to read the war diaries, signals, orders, and later interviews of the senior German commanders in Normandy is again to recognize the parallel with Alamein, as Rommel, having left France for a vacation with his wife in June 1944, was urgently sum-moned back to direct the counter-invasion—yet was still unable to convince his superiors that Normandy was not a feint, and was there-fore forced to keep his primary armored and infantry forces in re-serve in the Pas de Calais. Having failed to "Dunkirk" the Allied assault in Normandy, Rommel had been forced into a policy of firefighting, as on the Miteriya Ridge at Alamein; in other words, to react to each Anglo-Canadian threat around Caen with the remnants of his armored divisions, but never halting the expansion of the American sector behind, in the Cherbourg peninsula.

As German casualties had mounted it had become increasingly clear that, unless Hitler allowed his forces to withdraw to the Seine, they would be destroyed. As at Alamein, Hitler had refused. Thus the Allied radio communications decoding center at Bletchley Park—the unique "listening ear" of Ultra—could now see for itself the success of Montgomery's tactics, as the Führer hysterically ordered his German commanders to counterattack—culminating in his directive to try to cut off the neck of the American breakout at Mortain, east of Avranches.

Hitler's orders on August 2 reflected a belated realization on the German side that the eruption of the Allied volcano was taking place at the western end of the American line, not in the British and Canadian sector in the east. But it was too late. "All available panzer units, regardless of their present commitment, are to be taken from the other parts of the Normandy front, joined together under one specially qualified panzer operations staff, and sent into a concentrated attack as soon as possible," Hitler's orders ran. "The outcome of the whole campaign in France depends on the success of this attack."[16]

Von Kluge, however, as both supreme commander and commander of Army Group B, could not comply—for his main panzer elements were tied down attempting to hold back the British and Canadians near Caen. "Tanks are the backbone of our defense," von Kluge signaled back, adding, "Where they are withdrawn our front [facing the British and Canadians] will give way." He ended by warning that, if he was forced to mount the attack and it failed, "catastrophe will be inevitable."[17]

Hitler insisted nevertheless—and the German counterattack *did* go ahead, on August 6, 1944, employing elements of four panzer divisions. Only one was fresh, however. With some last-minute forewarning from Ultra, but mostly by dint of extraordinary bravery on the part of 30th U.S. Division at Hill 317, and punishing air support from General Quesada's 9th U.S. Tactical Air Force and the RAF's 2nd Tactical Air Force, General Collins easily held the offensive in 1st U.S. Army's sector—while Patton's 3rd U.S. Army armored divisions continued to uncurl to the south and east.

Thereafter, the Battle of Normandy became a German rout, with Patton's advance columns streaking through deserted terrain to the east, from Laval to Le Mans to Orleans and Chartres, while the German armored and infantry divisions found themselves caught in a trap at Falaise: the newly formed 1st Canadian Army under General Harry Crerar and Dempsey's 2nd British Army pounding them from the north, while 1st U.S. Army and 3rd U.S. Army attacked them from the south—and overhead, the Allied air forces pounded them from the skies.

Suddenly all the bickering and rear-headquarters intrigue were silenced. Although later historians would claim that the Allies had failed to close the Falaise gap completely, thus allowing considerable German forces to escape, this was an exaggeration—indeed the total number of tanks the Germans were able to save, from the entire Normandy campaign, was about sixty, while few combat soldiers crossed the Seine with more than their rifles. By August 15 the Allies had captured over 140,000 German troops; and on August 17 Hitler dismissed von Kluge, who then committed suicide. A week later, on August 24, 1944, Patton's first troops (General LeClerc's French 2nd Armored Division, which had refused to fight at Falaise) were in Paris, and by August 25 the entire Seine below Paris was in Allied hands, after 80 days of fighting—ten fewer than General Montgomery had estimated in his D-Day briefings.

While Montgomery was simplistic in stating afterwards that D-Day and the Battle of Normandy had gone exactly "according to plan"— which, being familiar with the details, he knew it certainly hadn't— the overall battle had, in the end, proceeded almost exactly as he had anticipated and hoped, with the Germans fiercely defending the direct route from Normandy to Paris, while the Americans wheeled around the German armies to the south and then to the east. By counterattacking at Mortain, Hitler had, moreover, unexpectedly played right into Montgomery's hands, allowing the Allies to entrap the larger part of the German armies in the Falaise pocket, sandwiched between the Anglo-Canadian and American armies, and pounded from the air until the area smelled like a charnel house. It is estimated that German casualties amounted to half a million men. Overlord had succeeded far beyond all Allied expectations.

For weeks SHAEF and the senior air commanders had complained at the slowness of Montgomery's tactical strategy. Now, however, with the total collapse of the German armed forces in Normandy ten days before the "due date," SHAEF found itself as wrong footed as the German high command—completely incapable of deciding how next to proceed, and stricken with what historian Stephen Ambrose later called "the victory disease." Instead of having prepared for their forthcoming role on the continent of Europe, its officers thus failed not only the test of history, but let down the brave soldiers, airmen, and sailors who had won the decisive battle of the west—the fruit of which would now be frittered away by SHAEF's unreadiness, lack of forward planning, failure to activate effective headquarters in France, inability to set a clear strategy to follow the seizure of the Rhine, and administrative planning chaos.

Montgomery had been (and would again be) charged with overcareful advance planning for D-Day and overcautious conduct of the Battle of Normandy; but he had, in the end, won the greatest Allied land battle of the war, and had done so ten days ahead of schedule. By contrast the supreme command headquarters' lack of a clearly stated strategy for a post-Normandy campaign was a scandal that was concealed at the time to preserve Allied unity, and afterwards in order to preserve the reputations of SHAEF's staff—from the supreme commander and his deputy down.

The Bridge Too Far

F OR YEARS Allied bombers had flown over Germany, attacking German communications, industrial complexes, and cities—without appreciable effect on Hitler's or the German populace's will to resist. Only by destroying the German armies on the ground, and definitively invading and occupying the Third Reich, could the Allies—both Russians and western Allies—bring Hitler's evil regime to an end and convince the German people that the Nazi game of military conquest and racial *Vernichtung*, or destruction, was up.

By which route, however, should the western Allies invade Germany, the field commanders in France and their staffs now asked? As Eisenhower's chief of staff admitted shortly after the war, the very decision to place the American armies on the right-hand flank of the D-Day invasion force had been dictated by their location in their training and assembly areas in the west of England. Had the American armies been on the Caen flank, they would, General Bedell-Smith confided to the American official military historians, have been in a better position to drive *northwards* into the heart of Germany, which "was already set through the Low Countries and the North of the Ruhr. The Low Countries were the logical route," he admitted, "but the British were never strong enough to make the main effort."[1]

Knowing that 21 Army Group would not be able to carry out this "main effort" on the "logical route" into Germany without American help, Montgomery had already become concerned about the next battle even before the Falaise battle was won. Thus on August 15, before the pocket was sealed, he sent an urgent confidential signal to Field-Marshal Brooke, rehearsing his own views on the next step to be taken in Allied ground strategy, while the German armies were in chaos: "After crossing Seine 12 and 21 Army Groups should keep together as a solid mass of some 40 divisions which should be so strong that it need fear nothing."[2] This vast Allied army should race north to seize Antwerp, and as it did so, capture Hitler's "terror weapons"—the V1 launching pads in the Pas de Calais. Its American right flank would run through the Ardennes, with its left-hand U.S. divisions seizing "Brussels, Aachen and Cologne," ready to seize the Ruhr from the north. Monty explained that he'd spoken to General Bradley, and "Bradley agrees entirely with above conception"[3]—a conception that fully accorded with original strategic expectations of SHAEF (Supreme Headquarters Allied Expeditionary Force) regarding the "logical route" into Germany.

Did Bradley really agree, though? Bradley, only days into his new role as an army group commander and beset with key decisions regarding the seizure of Brittany, the closing of the Falaise gap, and the thrust to Paris and the Seine, probably had simply not had time to consider future alternatives—leaving the matter to Eisenhower, as supreme commander.

It was certainly high time that Eisenhower, so impatient for "gains" in Normandy, address the issue, now that the breakout had taken place and a great victory was being won. With two million Allied soldiers fighting in Normandy and another (now unnecessary and distracting) Allied army that had landed near Marseilles on August 15 in the revived Operation Anvil, Eisenhower at last confirmed his decision to personally take over field command of the Allied armies at the end of August. However, with regard to the strategy his ground forces would follow beyond the Seine, he remained silent. He had received no directive from the Combined Chiefs of Staff on the matter, and although his planners had formulated a four-option scenario in May 1944, Eisenhower himself held no fixed idea of how or where he wished to proceed. Instead, he asked his subordinate commanders what they thought—"collecting ideas" as Monty described it a few days later.[4] This was democratic leadership, but of a kind unlikely to defeat the Germans, who were masters of clear-cut battlefield command and defensive warfare.

As the days went by, Bradley became confused. His 1st and 3rd U.S. Armies were racing northeast and eastward. Patton—his former commanding officer, now his subordinate—said he favored making a thrust to Metz and the Saar while the region was virtually denuded of German troops—indeed he was furious at SHAEF's idea that, in order to pursue the "logical route" into Germany, they might bow to British pressure and leave the eastern route via Frankfurt unexploited.

Montgomery, meanwhile, was driven to the brink of insubordination, indeed mild insanity. He had earlier remarked during the Falaise battle that Eisenhower's "ignorance as to how to run a war is absolute and complete; he has all the popular cries, but nothing else"[5]—a savage indictment, but one which didn't come near expressing the frustration he now felt at the impending loss of Allied strategic initiative through indecision and growing dispersion of effort. Eisenhower's inability to lay down a clear Allied strategy was, Monty felt, an insult to the profession of arms, as well as to those who had fallen in Normandy.

Behind the scenes, as the Allied troops continued to overrun and destroy the once-mighty Wehrmacht in France, the arguments went back and forth. Finally, on August 19, with Eisenhower still dithering over the question of the best route by which to invade Germany, Patton changed his mind! This time he backed Montgomery's plan—suggesting, however, that he repeat the role he had played in Normandy by crossing the Seine and then swinging his 3rd U.S. Army in another left-hook or end-run northwards, right up to the English Channel, cutting off all those surviving German troops that were retreating from Falaise and the Caen area. Patton had the proposal, "Plan A," hand-delivered to Bradley's headquarters.

In one of the worst but least-known strategic blunders of World

War II, Bradley and Eisenhower nixed Patton's new plan in favor of the one he had earlier proposed: that the American army group prepare itself to exploit the absence of German forces east of Paris, and push on via Metz and the Saar to Frankfurt.

It was thus from that day, August 19, 1944, that Allied high command, in the moment of Montgomery's great victory in Normandy, began to fall apart. Tactical victory of an almost unimaginable dimension turned into strategic failure of an almost unimaginable kind—opening a potentially disastrous rift between the British and American approaches to the defeat of Germany.

Could this strategic policy crisis have been avoided? To what extent was Montgomery himself responsible for the problem by virtue of his insistence on Allied cohesion, concentration, and the Schwerpunkt, rather than dispersion?

Conversely, to what extent did Eisenhower's inability to make up his mind as Allied supreme commander doom the Allies to a "winter of discontent"—culminating in a German counteroffensive that, a few months later, sliced through his American armies in the Ardennes?

These and other aspects of the role of the western Allies in World War II will be debated for the rest of time. Certainly Montgomery knew from his experience in the Mediterranean—the campaign in North Africa; the planning for Husky; the failure to stop the German garrison from evacuating from Sicily; the planning of the main Allied landing at Salerno (and the mad plan to drop a lightly-armed U.S. airborne division outside Rome, almost a year before the city fell to the Allies); the lack of overall tactical strategy in the campaign in Italy; and the failure of Eisenhower's planned landing at Anzio—that Eisenhower was unlikely to perform any better in northwestern Europe. But with the benefit of hindsight, given what followed, would it not have been better for Montgomery simply to have carried out whatever orders Eisenhower gave, without question—and to have attempted to live with the consequences, however disappointing or even disastrous?

How, though, could Montgomery have done so, as a general who respected his German foe and who knew how hard it was to beat him

WORLD WAR I. Severely wounded in the trenches on the western front in October 1914, Montgomery returned to France as a Brigade-Major fifteen months later, serving in almost all the major battles thereafter, and ending World War I as chief of staff of a division. Here he poses with his brother Donald (left), who was serving in a Canadian division. "At plain straightforward fighting," he wrote of the Canadian soldiers, "they are magnificent"—but they "forget that the whole art of war is to gain your objective with as little loss as possible." The gentleman in the center is unidentified. *Private collection*

INFANTRY BATTALION COMMANDER. Between the two world wars promotion in the British army—as in the U.S. army—was desperately slow. Thanks to his insubordinate, know-it-all personality, Montgomery was lucky to be given command of his regiment, the 1st Battalion of the Royal Warwickshires, with whom he had first served as a subaltern on the northwest frontier of India. Here, mounted, Lieutenant-Colonel Montgomery parades his battalion before maneuvers near the famous pyramids of Giza, while serving in the British army's Canal Brigade in 1933. *Private collection*

MONTY IN MOURNING.
Montgomery, who was inept and awkward with women, found eleven years of happiness between 1926 and 1937 when he married a WWI widow with two children, Betty Carver, an artist. He took her everywhere with him—throughout the Middle East and India—and had a son, David, by her. Just as Brigadier Montgomery was conducting maneuvers to decide if he was fit to become a major-general Betty was stung by an insect and died of septicemia. Montgomery was inconsolable and dedicated himself to preparations for the coming war. *Imperial War Museum*

BEFORE DUNKIRK. The British Expeditionary Force, under General Lord Gort, was sent to France to meet Hitler's expected German invasion soon after the declaration of war in September 1939. Here Montgomery shows a British continuation of the Maginot line, which he criticized as "useless," to the Minister of War and Lord Gort—whom he also criticized as "useless." *Imperial War Museum*

ARRIVAL IN EGYPT. "Fit and fresh—new brains on an old problem," Monty later wrote of his appointment in August 1942 to command the British 8th Army, under a new Middle East C-in-C in Cairo, General Alexander. The "old problem" was Rommel—who had run 8th Army fifteen hundred miles back across the desert almost to the Nile by the summer of 1942. For a while it seemed possible the entire Middle East, with its precious oil and Suez Canal, would fall under German control. *Imperial War Museum*

DESERT VICTORY. Anxious whether to reinforce defeat by sending American equipment and launching an invasion of Morocco and Algeria, President Roosevelt sent his former Republican opponent, Wendell Willkie, as his personal envoy to Africa and the Middle East in August 1942. Willkie was the first major American figure to visit General Montgomery in the field of battle—sending back glowing reports of Monty's first victory over Rommel at Alam Halfa, on September 5, 1942, six weeks before the decisive Battle of Alamein. *Imperial War Museum*

MONTY IN ITALY. Allied strategic military planning for a war on the Italian mainland was nothing less than a disgrace in Montgomery's eyes. His 8th Army was ferried across the Messina Straits at Reggio on September 3, 1943. Meanwhile, 350 miles further north, General Clark was ordered to land with 5th U.S. Army at Salerno, near Naples—where the Germans were waiting with a trap. Only Clark's last-minute use of American paratroopers, and German concern that Montgomery's 8th Army, fighting northward, would strike the Wehrmacht defenders in the rear, saved the Allies from catastrophe. *Imperial War Museum*

WHO WILL COMMAND OVERLORD? After the surrender of the Italian armies and the securing of the Foggia airfields for U.S. heavy bomber groups in September 1943, there seemed to Monty no point in fighting in Italy, but Churchill insisted—resulting in sad and unnecessary British and American casualties. Monty therefore prayed that Field-Marshal Sir Alan Brooke, seen here visiting Monty and Alex in Italy on December 14, 1943, would choose him rather than Alexander to lead the D-Day armies for the invasion of France in 1944. *Imperial War Museum*

ALLIED LAND FORCE COMMANDER. As commander in chief of the four Allied armies designated for D-Day and the invasion of France, Monty's role was not only to prepare the plans for the greatest amphibious invasion in human history, but also to lead in the field the men who would have to win victory in the subsequent land battle. Unlike WWI commanders he made it his task to visit and inspire every single soldier who would be crossing the English Channel, in groups of 5,000. *Imperial War Museum*

CHURCHILL'S VISIT. Inspired by Montgomery's new broom as C-in-C of all Allied Land Forces preparing to invade France, Prime Minister Winston Churchill switched from defeatism (nightmares of the Dardanelles in 1915 and the disastrous Anglo-French landings in Norway in 1940) to exuberant excitement. By May 1944 Churchill, who loved to meddle in details, had become impossible—and during a visit to Montgomery's headquarters Montgomery had to threaten to resign unless the Prime Minister stopped interfering. *Imperial War Museum*

D-DAY COMMANDER. As commander in chief in the field, Montgomery commanded both the Allied armies landing on June 6, 1944: Gen. Miles Dempsey's 2nd British Army, and Gen. Omar Bradley's 1st U.S. Army. Here, in a field in Normandy, Montgomery confers with Bradley and Dempsey, just four days after the D-Day triumph. *Imperial War Museum*

PLANNING THE BREAK-OUT. Monty and Patton had been fellow army commanders in the invasion of Sicily in 1943. "A great general," Monty would say of the impetuous Patton, "[but he could] ruin your battle in an afternoon." Both Bradley and Montgomery were adamant that Patton, shown here visiting Monty's headquarters on July 7, 1944, should not take command of the highly mobile 3rd U.S. Army until American heavy bombers and Bradley's 1st U.S. Army had first broken the back of German opposition in the *bocage*, while the British 2nd Army held off the bulk of German armor around Caen. *Imperial War Museum*

THE BATTLE FOR CAEN. Caen, on the Allied eastern flank, was intended by Montgomery to be the British and Canadian hinge upon which the American invasion force would swing—fighting its way south to the Loire and only then northward towards the Seine. Only when visiting Monty and the ruins of the city did Churchill realize how tough was Montgomery's task in holding Hitler's armored divisions on the eastern flank, while American forces prepared to make the southern break-out. *Imperial War Museum*

IKE TAKES OVER. As supreme commander, Eisenhower had to ensure the overall air, sea, and ground performance of the second front. When on August 23, 1944, Eisenhower told Monty in person that he would take field command of all Allied army groups in Normandy, in addition to his other responsibilities, Montgomery—who favored a massive, single-thrust beyond the Seine to the Ruhr to finish the war in 1944—was devastated. *Imperial War Museum*

THE BATTLE OF THE BULGE. Charged with rescuing the broken 1st U.S. Army front, where an entire group of German Panzer armies had broken through the American line and were making for Liege, Montgomery took immediate command of two U.S. armies for the first time in American history in the midst of a battle. His generals (seen here on December 28, 1944) thought it his finest hour. However, his tactless humiliation of beleaguered General Bradley, and refusal to turn the defensive battle into an offensive campaign in strategically worthless terrain, destroyed his reputation in the United States. *Imperial War Museum*

FIELD-MARSHAL MONTGOMERY. As commander in chief of the Allied land forces for the invasion of Normandy, and having commanded the Allies' northern armies in the subsequent conquest of Nazi Germany, Montgomery was painted by Frank O. Salisbury in 1945 in his distinctive black beret with two badges as the First Soldier of Europe. *National Portrait Gallery, London*

in battle? Montgomery's "legend" was built upon the fact that he cared about the lives and welfare of his men, and refused to put them into battle unless he had done his best to make sure they would win by having a clear plan, good staff work, robust commanders, logistical backup, interservice support, and a commander who would never pass the initiative to the enemy. He therefore objected to Eisenhower's latest proposal that the two army groups—Anglo-Canadian and American—now split apart, the one driving north to Antwerp and Cologne, the other to Metz and Frankfurt. Fighting the Germans, he pointed out to Eisenhower, was a "full-time job"— and he begged Eisenhower to allow him to continue to command both groups as single Allied ground force commander, with a clear mandate to command a single, massive Allied thrust through the Low Countries into northern Germany. He even said he would gladly serve under General Bradley if Eisenhower preferred to put Bradley in charge of it.

Eisenhower could not suddenly change his spots any more than Montgomery. He understood the superiority of Monty's counter-proposal for field command, but he could not agree to it. His boss, General Marshall, would never accept a "Brit" remaining in command of the American armies on the battlefield of France and northwestern Europe, when the preponderance of American military force was growing daily. After the disappointingly slow advance in the bocage, Bradley and Patton were performing brilliantly in the Allied advance to the Seine—yet to promote Bradley for a second time in as many weeks, when his own SHAEF staff were urging him to take field command himself, was more than Eisenhower was willing to brave. He therefore passed up the opportunity—and the struggle for Eisenhower's ear now began in earnest.

Some commanders, like certain presidents and prime ministers, use their authority to pursue committee-like consensus, using their own personal skills to achieve it. Such a commander was Dwight D. Eisenhower—and his skills at handling prima donna subordinate commanders such as Patton and Montgomery would make him one of the outstanding remote headquarters Allied commanders in chief in history. Yet that place in the history of war was predicated on the frontline battlefield success of his prima donnas in saving him from his own command failures—prima donnas who despised Eisenhower's battlefield ignorance yet admired him as a boss and felt they had to win his field campaigns both for and in spite of him. To his credit, Eisenhower knew and accepted this. It was for this reason that, where others called for the head of Patton after the slapping incident in Sicily, or for Monty's removal during the "sticky" fighting in Normandy, he never dared sack or remove them. Fighting the Germans, Eisenhower recognized, was a tough business, for which tough, battlefield generals were required, and he was not one of them.

Had Eisenhower accepted Patton's Plan A on August 19, 1944, a week before the fall of Paris, World War II might have well been won that year—as Eisenhower had placed a bet with Montgomery that it would be. Or if Bradley had declared his own preference for a unified thrust to the north, with its right flank on the Ardennes—whether commanded in the field by Eisenhower, Montgomery, or Bradley—the Allies might have avoided the nonsense that now ensued, with each Army group commander pursuing his own axis of advance towards Germany. But it was not to be.

For Montgomery this was the worst moment of the war, in the middle of its very best moment, the climax of Overlord. Montgomery's letters, diary, and recorded conversations of this period testify to a frustration bordering on rage. With two U.S. armies under his command as well as one British and one Canadian army, he had just won one of the great battles of modern history, defeating Hitler's vaunted forces in the west—armies that had once Dunkirked the French and British armies in 1940. Now, with their forces racing for the Seine, the Allied armies had only to get the next step right, by keeping their forces concentrated in a massive race to the Ruhr via Aachen, and they would be threatening the industrial heart of Germany within weeks. Instead, on September 4, 1944, Eisenhower announced that he would try to do everything, simultaneously: send British forces north to capture the vital port of Antwerp, secure the V1 rocket sites, liberate Belgium, and strike towards the Ruhr via the Aachen gap, while in the east he would direct his American forces towards

Frankfurt via the Metz gap, "practically on the flank of the forces that would advance straight eastward through Aachen," as Eisenhower noted on September 5.[6]

Montgomery was appalled. Such forces would *not* be "practically on the flank" of each other; they would be separated by the Ardennes, through which Hitler had smashed his armored forces in May 1940. Unfortunately, Field-Marshal Brooke had left London to visit the British forces in Italy and then sail with the prime minister across the Atlantic to meet with President Roosevelt and the Combined Chiefs of Staff off the coast of Canada; this left no one of political or military stature in England to guide Monty.

Once before, in North Africa, Montgomery had "piped down" and let others lead, providing the best of his 8th Army formations for the finale of the campaign: the attack on Tunis, which ended "the business." Had he been ordered by Brooke to pipe down and simply assist an American thrust to Frankfurt, spearheaded by General Patton, he would have complied, however reluctantly. Indeed as the weeks went by, he would suggest such an alternative, eastward-thrust strategy, despite his deeper conviction that it was northern, not southern Germany that would have to be seized to end German resistance. What mattered most, in his view, was that in whichever direction the thrust was made, it be massive and concentrated so that it "need fear nothing"; the Allies should not press forward on *all* fronts, with no overwhelming strength anywhere.

It was in this Allied command vacuum, with Eisenhower splitting the Allied axis of advance with the intention of reinforcing whichever one prospered, that Montgomery railed against his supreme commander. He warned that, with the Canadian army dedicated to seizing the crucial Pas de Calais seaports (which it did in September) he did not have the resources in 2nd British Army to carry out his proposed assignment in Belgium without exposing his right flank—as had happened when the French and British forces moved into Belgium on May 10, 1940.

Since taking over from Montgomery on September 1 Eisenhower had become the new Allied ground commander, but—in headquarters still situated on the western shores of the Cherbourg peninsula at Granville, even farther than London from the front lines—was torn between American opportunism and British logic. Once again, he tried to defer making an unequivocal decision. Knowing how important was the seizure of Belgium's great sea-terminal at Antwerp, and reluctantly accepting Monty's argument that 2nd British Army would need American divisions to strengthen its right flank, he agreed to furnish a limited number of divisions from Hodges' 1st U.S. Army for the purpose—though he made clear that Hodges would remain under command of General Bradley, whose main thrust, under the leadership of General Patton, would drive east, towards Metz.

It was in this way that Eisenhower's initial decision to split the army groups into a British and an American axis had effectively evolved into *three* thrusts. Bradley, his American army group commander, would command two of them, in the north *and* the east, separated by the Ardennes. South of Bradley's army group, the forces that had carried out Anvil would then join a *fourth*, American-French army group under the U.S. general Jacob Devers to form a line further south that would make a third thrust. Thus, Allied forces would be stretched from Antwerp to the Swiss border, as in World War I, in what Eisenhower proudly called the "broad front" but was in reality a patchwork line so long that the Allies simply did not have enough troops for it.

In the fog not only of war but of postwar historiography, the Allied strategic tragedy of late August 1944 would generate a welter of accusation and counter-accusation larded with nationalistic and personality differences.

Genial, intelligent, high-minded (and, after the war, a two-term, much-loved Republican U.S. president), General Eisenhower came off best in the majority of such historical accounts, for it was hard even for the most patriotic of British military historians not to feel sympathy for a supreme commander carrying so many responsibilities—political and military, international and national—as well as dealing with prima donna after prima donna. As the interface between the Combined Chiefs of Staff, a role that entailed daily communications from General Marshall in Washington and incessant phone calls and even personal visits with Prime Minister Churchill in London, Eisenhower (and his staff) certainly fulfilled the political and personality-control aspects of his supreme command role better than any conceivable alternative figure could have. After all, even Hitler had had to dismiss his vastly more professional successive "supreme commanders" in Normandy—von Rundstedt and von Kluge— just as Churchill had had to dismiss his successive supreme commanders in the Middle East before Alamein. In this sense, Eisenhower had *survived* where others hadn't—from the invasion of North Africa to the triumph in Normandy—and he was justly lauded for his patience and dedication to the Allied cause.

Yet as good as his overall performance was, Eisenhower's leadership in terms of field command was, were truth to be told, lamentable. Had the D-Day landings failed—as he later admitted they might well have done without Montgomery's leadership—both Eisenhower and Churchill, the prime minister had warned, probably would have been relieved of their jobs. And, had Montgomery and Patton not saved the situation in the Battle of the Bulge in the winter of 1944–45, Eisenhower would probably have been dismissed or forced to take a field deputy to take command of the broken Allied land armies. In other words, Eisenhower needed great field generals to win his battles, for the business of fighting the Germans was not his forté.

Working in tandem, Montgomery and Patton had conquered Sicily in thirty-eight days. Now, in the summer of 1944, under Monty's leadership they had conquered the combined German armies in Normandy in only eighty days. In retrospect, it is clear that Eisenhower had only to keep these two greatest of Allied field generals fighting in the same battle to be assured of victory. By neglecting to do so, Eisenhower missed his chance of attaining true military, rather than politico-military, greatness.

By authorizing Patton to drive eastward, but starving him of sufficient fuel and logistical backup to ensure the success of his thrust into southern Germany, Eisenhower doomed the American drive towards Frankfurt, which soon came to grief near Metz. Moreover, in the Allied center, the limited divisions of 1st U.S. Army also found themselves becoming bogged down before Aachen. And north of

Brussels, after a brilliant tank breakout that took British armor right to the docks of Antwerp on September 3, 1944, the British 2nd Army also would become bogged down.

For Montgomery—who had been promoted to field-marshal on September 1, 1944, in recognition of his triumph on the field of battle—this was exactly what he had feared: dispersion of Allied effort, with no one thrust strong enough to break through the stiffening German defenses, backed by the Siegfried Line. In fact, unknown to the Allies, Hitler was not only ordering his generals to halt the Allied advances that were so spread out; he was also beginning his own preparations for a massive armored counterattack through the Ardennes in December 1944, one that would split open the Allied front line, just as the Germans had done in May 1940.

It was in concern over this "broad-front" loss of Allied initiative, therefore, that Montgomery ordered the fateful airborne *coup de main* assault across the Rhine, in the far north of the Allied line, beyond the unfinished German Siegfried Line defenses—hoping to obtain a bridgehead over the crucial river before winter, and get troops into a position from which (as in Normandy after D-Day) to expand and build up the bridgehead before breaking out into the plains of northern Germany and seizing the Ruhr: Operation Market Garden.

The day British tanks and trucked infantry seized Antwerp, a smaller version of this *coup de main* plan had been hatched in outline at Monty's request between 21 Army Group headquarters and the headquarters of the new Allied Airborne Army headquarters under General Brereton.[7] This plan would have had small, brigade-size, lightly-armed paratroop drops start on September 7, to capture, from the air, a series of bridges across the Maas, Waal, and Rhine Rivers as the British 2nd Army continued its helter-skelter advance northwards. (During the Battle of Normandy a number of such assault-drops had been planned to take place at Caen, at Falaise, and, later on, at the Seine. All had been cancelled, either because the lightly armed airborne troops would incur too many casualties behind enemy lines, because anti-aircraft fire was too heavy, or—as in the final phase of the Battle of Normandy—because events simply made such plans redundant.)

Now, in the first week of September 1944, with German defenses on the Albert Canal north of Brussels halting the British advance, the notion of small airdrops on the Dutch bridges leading to Arnhem seemed inappropriate to Montgomery's main headquarters staff, setting up their offices in Brussels. There was no way in which 2nd Army's ground forces would be able to reach the paratroopers without first bringing up massive reinforcements and bridging equipment, they pointed out. Thus General Dempsey turned his eyes instead to Wesel, on the direct route to the Ruhr, where he hoped he could obtain an alternative bridgehead across the Rhine.

The Rhine, however, was Europe's mightiest river. Crossing it against stalwart German defense would be akin to a mini–D-Day operation, requiring sufficient airborne troops, close air support, training, and logistical backup to maintain the bridgehead, if passage were won. Air Marshal Leigh-Mallory had been ordered to the Far East, and no replacement air force commander in chief had been appointed by Eisenhower to support the armies. Air Marshal Tedder, the deputy supreme commander, and the air barons all declared that the density of anti-aircraft fire at Wesel would make airborne landings and even close air support impossible.

Thus, *faute de mieux*, the notion of an airdrop at Arnhem was resurrected as a possibility, provided the Allied Airborne Army and 2nd Army could mount the operation to "bounce the Rhine" with sufficient strength and in time to beat arriving German reinforcements.

Though many military historians have applauded Arnhem as perhaps the boldest Allied air assault of World War II, it was, in almost every respect—strategic, tactical, intelligence, logistical, personal—a complete disaster, not only wiping out the entire British 1st Airborne division, but giving the British a precarious peninsula of marshy land in the heart of Holland that was difficult to hold, and that led nowhere because the bridge at Arnhem was bravely won but soon lost.

Operation Market Garden was launched on September 17, 1944, but after the two American airborne divisions succeeded brilliantly in capturing and holding their targeted bridges over the Maas and Waal until ground forces were able to relieve them, the northern armies were doomed to holding a thin, pencil-like corridor through the low polders for the next six months—a corridor that was strategically irrelevant. Arnhem would not be recaptured by the Allies until April 1945.

Of all the battles that Bernard Montgomery commanded, Arnhem, the "Bridge Too Far," was the most heart-breaking: the one most poorly conceived, most poorly planned, most poorly supported from the air, and the one that would be the most pointless unless *entirely* successful—which it wasn't. Montgomery had always taught that senior commanders were responsible to their men for the battles they asked them to undertake. At Arnhem he suffered his worst defeat since Dunkirk, as the bravest of British paratroopers seized and held onto the vital bridge at Arnhem for thirty-six hours, but when no ground forces arrived to relieve them, were inevitably killed or captured by the Germans, who had a panzer corps refitting in the vicinity.

As the last few surviving British paratroopers swam back across the Rhine at Oosterbeck on the night of September 25, 1944, Montgomery had to accept that he had squandered his chance of keeping the initiative; that, instead of attacking so far north, he should have established a defensive line, while offering General Hodges' 1st U.S. Army flanking support for its thrust towards Aachen. The main tasks of this defensive line would have been ensuring that the north bank of the Scheldt estuary was seized so that vital Allied supply vessels could safely approach Antwerp, and cutting off the escape route of the tens of thousands of German troops retreating before the Canadian army on the coast.

Now, however, it was too late.

Worse still, Montgomery began to intrigue behind Eisenhower's back to have Brooke and Churchill press for him to be given command of the northern front as far as Aachen, which would give him enough troops to regenerate his thrust northeastward to the Ruhr, since General Bradley seemed wedded now to Patton's eastward drive toward Frankfurt. Such behavior was disloyal, insubordinate, and unrealistic by this point. Getting Antwerp open, in order to guarantee supplies through the coming winter, was far more important. At a remote headquarters conference called by Eisenhower on October 5, 1944, (which Monty had been compelled to attend, as his British boss, Field-Marshal Brooke, was there), Admiral Ramsay duly "lambasted" Monty for "not having made the capture of Antwerp the immediate objective at the highest level." "I feel that Monty's strategy for once is at fault," Brooke noted in his diary that night. "Instead of carrying out the advance on Arnhem he ought to have made certain of Antwerp in the first place."[8]

Had Montgomery, like Leigh-Mallory (who died in a plane crash), been moved at this juncture to another theater of war, and had his replacement accepted that the increasing preponderance of American troops and matériel would inevitably push British and Canadian forces in northwestern Europe into a subordinate role, the Allies would undoubtedly have had northern Europe's biggest and most important port in working order within weeks of Antwerp's capture. Worse still, the need to maintain the British "corridor" leading up to, but not into, Arnhem left Montgomery with insufficient British forces to take over sections of the extended American line.

Instead, Monty remained and continued to do what he never tolerated on the part of his own subordinates—he "bellyached." Indeed, so impossible did Montgomery become, that on October 13, 1944, Eisenhower was driven to recommend that either Montgomery or he be removed—preparing a signal to the General Marshall and the Combined Chiefs of Staff to that effect.

Could Eisenhower have managed without Montgomery, after the failure of Market Garden? Many officers at SHAEF thought so— enough, certainly, for Montgomery to apologize abjectly on October 14, before SHAEF could dispatch the "him or me" signal. He promised Eisenhower the supreme commander would "hear no more from me on the subject of command" and that he would have the port of Antwerp working *instanter*.

In fact it was another month before the Canadian troops were able to secure the Scheldt approaches. (The first ships unloaded at the end of November 1944.) In the meantime, Montgomery's problem was not only that he had gotten too big for his British boots in a campaign increasingly dominated by the U.S. military, but that his British boots had become patently too small for what he wanted to do—with word coming from the war office that he should begin returning British divisions to England to be sent out to the Far East, where the British were seeking to drive the Japanese out of Burma.

With Patton stalled for months around Metz, suffering 47,000 casualties in fruitless battles from September to mid-December in an offense that only advanced the American line by twenty-five miles, and with 1st and 9th U.S. Armies slogging through the Hürtgen Forest to the Roer dams and suffering more than 57,000 casualties (with another 50,000 men reporting sick), the situation was in every way galling. In Monty's opinion, he had demonstrated the kind of field command that could beat the Germans in open battle with sufficient forces. Yet such forces were not provided, and without them, against soldiers as professional in defense as the Germans, he could do nothing; his British barrel was empty. He would have to accept a reduced role as a junior team player, no longer as the team captain.

Instead of meekly swallowing this pill, however, as he had promised he would do, Montgomery soon began to wage, behind the scenes, a renewed campaign of denigration of General Eisenhower, his superior officer and the supreme Allied commander, as well as Eisenhower's "useless" deputy supreme commander, Air Marshal Tedder. In place of Tedder, Montgomery argued, the Allies must appoint a full-time, no-nonsense field deputy or commander, who would take a grip on the campaign before matters went seriously wrong.

Such backbiting was perhaps no worse than the backstabbing Eisenhower's headquarters had indulged in during the epic Battle of Normandy, but the perpetrators had in SHAEF's case not been criticizing their superior officer. Montgomery's criticism of his direct American superior was rank insubordination, and it was counterproductive. Eisenhower had many responsibilities in marrying both supreme and ground force commands on behalf of the Allies, but he certainly had no intention of taking a British field commander, or, indeed, an American as his deputy. Warned by Montgomery that

Bradley's troops in the Ardennes were perilously weak, Eisenhower passed on the advice to Bradley, but did nothing more. Thus, when Hitler's great counteroffensive kicked off on the morning of December 16, 1944, it was like Pearl Harbor, but on land: Bradley's forces in the Ardennes were completely unprepared for the onslaught.

The Battle of the Bulge

"P ARDON MY French . . . but where in hell has this son of a bitch gotten all his strength?"[1] Bradley would eventually ask, as the magnitude of the German counteroffensive in the Ardennes became clear.

Hitler had ordered absolute secrecy in preparing his armored counterattack. Allied intelligence had come to rely on Ultra for advance warning of a German riposte—and since there was no reference in German signals to the impending operation in the Ardennes, Operation "Wacht am Rhein" hit the Allies like a thunderbolt.

Eisenhower and Bradley were playing bridge together outside Paris on the evening of the attack. In retrospect it would be the worst moment of their lives: losing control of a battle they never really understood, and which they certainly had no ability to command.

All Eisenhower—his tactical headquarters at Rheims and his main SHAEF (Supreme Headquarters Allied Expeditionary Force) headquarters back in Versailles—could do was alert his two lightly armed Allied airborne formations for possible fighting, while Bradley reassigned his only two reserve divisions—one from General Simpson's 9th U.S. and one from Patton's 3rd U.S. Army—to reinforce Hodges's

1st U.S. Army in Ardennes. Once those reserves were alerted, there did not seem much more that either could do but wait and see. After replacing Montgomery as ground forces commander in chief at the end of August 1944, Eisenhower had only toured his extended front line *once*. It was now December 16. He had no system of liaison officers; and his communications were so deficient that it would take days to get signals to and from his own commanders in the field.

Bradley initially thought the German assault was merely a spoiling attack designed to delay Patton's impending offensive in the Saar. Eisenhower instinctively felt it to be more serious, but had no idea what to do to meet it. Only twice had he suffered such a surprise attack. The first time had been at Kasserine, early in 1943, a German attack that had been too modest to do more than give the green forces of a single American corps a rude shock; then at Mortain on August 6, 1944, an American corps had been attacked by 140 tanks and elements drawn from four divisions, but Bradley's forces, under General Collins, had repulsed it without difficulty with the aid of the Allied air forces.

This time, however, instead of four under-strength German divisions operating at the extremity of long lines of communication strung across France, the attack had sprung from the heart of Germany with ten times as many panzers as at Mortain and with two thousand guns. Twenty-eight German divisions—twelve of them panzer divisions—were on the warpath in weather that precluded Allied air attack and in territory that made swift reinforcement of the Allied positions impossible.

The true story of the Battle of the Bulge—the extraordinary manner in which the German armed forces seized the tactical and strategic initiative from the Allies, the failure of Allied intelligence, the breakdown in Allied communications, the extent of Allied casualties, the panic induced by German assassination units operating behind the Allied lines, the breakdown of General Bradley's 12th U.S. Army command headquarters, and the failure of General Eisenhower as ground force commander in chief to heed Montgomery's warnings or maintain reserves against such an attack—was never addressed in post-war accounts of the battle, for it had been too humiliating a defeat for the Allies, coming so late in the war. Thus, while the "Bridge Too Far" would have a hundred historical post-mortems attempting to draw the lessons of such a brave but foolhardy Allied assault, the Battle of the Bulge went for the most part unrecorded and uncritically examined in the United States, save for understandably fulsome accounts of the great courage shown in defending St. Vith and Bastogne.

In reality Gen. Courtney Hodges's 1st U.S. Army, which bore the entire brunt of the German offensive, simply lacked a commander able to deal with such a massive enemy attack on his front. As the American military historian Russell Weigley later remarked, Hodges was "the model of a rumpled, assertive, small-town banker." Indeed, when German advance echelons came close to Hodges' headquarters at Spa, the banker and his staff simply fled their headquarters—leaving not only undestroyed top secret papers, maps, and equipment, but the largest stockpile of American fuel in the north! Communication with his front-line forces in 1st U.S. Army had in many cases already been severed, and when his entire headquarters decamped, Hodges lost almost all remaining communication with them, as well as with his boss General Bradley in Luxembourg, south of the German penetration.

Three days into the German onslaught, on December 19, with German forces bursting through the thinly-held American line and no sign that Hodges could stop them, General Eisenhower called a belated conference in Verdun, at which it was decided simply to "plug holes" on Hodges's front. Meanwhile Patton was ordered to cancel his impending 3rd U.S. Army attack in the Eiffel, hand over his Saar front to General Dever's 6th Army Group, switch his tank divisions north, and attack with six divisions the southern flank of the German salient, which was believed to be manned largely by infantry. Asked when he could launch such a counterattack, Patton said in "thirty-six hours," with three divisions. Fearing that such a hasty move would inevitably be too weak, Eisenhower and Bradley both told him to delay the attack until his divisions were assembled and could thrust hard through the German infantry units on the southern flank all the way to the panzer forces in the center, forcing them to halt their advance towards the Meuse. "Funny thing, George," Eisenhower, who had just been made a five-star general, joked to Patton, "every time I get a new star I get attacked." "And every time you get attacked," Patton responded as a three-star general, "I pull you out."[2]

Patton had anticipated such a request the day before, and full of bravado, he called his chief of staff and told him to order his divisions to turn north, where Patton would personally direct the attack, which was scheduled to kick off on December 23, in four days' time, a full *week* after the German attack had begun.

Meanwhile Montgomery's unique system of liaison officers was providing him with the only complete picture of the Allied front through which the Germans had been smashing their way. With growing concern Montgomery watched as German panzer divisions slammed through the snowbound American lines towards the Meuse—threatening, if successful, to drive through the British rear to the North Sea, as in 1940.

The amount of information coming out of SHAEF, as the supposed headquarters of the Allied ground force commander, was scandalously meager and out-of-date. No one knew anything for certain, and brave American troops were cut off and dying as a result. Because of the argument over single ground force command in September and October, Montgomery did not dare openly criticize what he saw as the inevitable consequence of Eisenhower's "broad front" approach to warfare: everyone attacking everywhere and no real reserves other than lightly armed airborne troops. But now that Bradley had lost touch with his own 1st U.S. Army commander and three German armies were smashing their way through Hodges's front in the Ardennes in weather that precluded Allied air attack, the situation was in danger of spiraling out of Allied control. Montgomery immediately took action to counter such a threat by pulling back a complete British corps into reserve and ordering British advance units to move into the rear of the American sector to guard the unmanned Meuse crossings lest advance parties of Germans capture them by *coup de main*. Finally, with no sign that Bradley was even in touch with Hodges, he urged SHAEF to allow him to take command of the battle and signaled his concerns to Field-Marshal Brooke, who spoke to Churchill.

Still, no one dared tell the supreme commander what he should do—or they did and were fired. Thus, on the night of December 19, 1944, after Eisenhower's return from Verdun, two of the most senior British officers at SHAEF went to Eisenhower's chief of staff, General Bedell-Smith, and told him the bitter truth. Almost twenty German divisions had already been identified in the German offensive, and there may have been more on the way. Unless Field-Marshal Montgomery was put in immediate command in the Ardennes, they argued, the Germans could win a great victory there, with terrible consequences for the Allied prosecution of the war.

So furious was General Bedell-Smith that he sacked both the officers forthwith—telling them to clear their desks and be out of the headquarters by midday on December 20. Had Bradley not claimed, at his morning conference at Versailles, that the German armored forces which had made the breakthrough were "relatively small" and that American disorganization had been "less than had been feared"?[3]

When the news came that Bradley had now lost touch completely with Hodges, and that the Germans were already within striking distance of the Meuse, hundreds of miles from Patton's proposed counterattack which would not begin for another three days—Bedell-Smith was forced to eat crow. With a heavy heart he told Eisenhower it was an "open-and-shut case": *they had failed to appreciate the magnitude of the German assault.* The supreme commander would have to swallow the bitter pill and call Montgomery. And tell Bradley.

With a sick stomach, Eisenhower asked for a call to be put through direct to Montgomery's tactical headquarters in Holland. Incredibly, it was only the second time he had spoken to Montgomery, his own 21 Army Group commander, in more than a month. He said he understood the Germans were in danger of breaking through to the Meuse, and he asked the field-marshal to take command of 1st and 9th U.S. Armies in the field and bring the German offensive to a halt.

Pretending that the line had then become too crackly to continue the conversation, Montgomery put the phone down. He had heard enough. "Kit!" he called to his military assistant. "I want the largest

Union Jack that will go on the bonnet [hood] of the car. Also eight motor-cycle outriders."[4] He was, he said, going to take charge—at the front.

In the opinion of Montgomery's first biographer, Alan Moorehead, this was Montgomery's finest hour—the summation of a lifetime's study and experience of field command. He had already met with his Canadian and British army commanders and explained the worsening situation in the American sector, telling them he still hoped there were sufficient American forces in the salient area to meet the German offensive without requiring troops from 21 Army Group, who were preparing to mount a crossing of the Rhine early in the new year. In case the Germans did break through, however, he ordered the British to be ready for a battle behind the Meuse and the Canadians to sidestep into British front-line positions in order to release more of Dempsey's 2nd British Army formations into reserve. This would delay preparations for the invasion of Germany, planned to set out from the Nijmegen area in Holland, but it had to be done.

For himself Monty was bursting with energy. "Like Christ come to cleanse the temple" was one officer's description of Montgomery's arrival at General Hodges's new headquarters at Chaudfontaine an hour later—for Montgomery radiated complete confidence, despite the severity of the situation. General Simpson, commanding the 9th U.S. Army to the north of the German salient, was also present, and gave his own report on the situation.

The Germans were reckoned to have amassed up to thirty divisions for their attack, but having commanded two million Allied troops in Normandy, Monty was unperturbed. Field-Marshal von Rundstedt, Montgomery's old adversary from Normandy, was once again the German commander in chief, or supreme commander, having been reappointed by Hitler after his dismissal of August 2. Having beaten von Rundstedt in Normandy as a general, Monty was certain he could do so again, as a British field-marshal now—indeed he relished the idea. The Americans had plenty of men, huge air forces, and plenty of matériel, from tanks to artillery and ammunition. It was time, he felt, to stop "frigging about"—to shorten the

Allied line and create reserves, not only in order to seal off the German breakthrough, but to retrieve and retain the Allied initiative
and make the German armies dance to the Allied tune, not vice versa.
His first orders, therefore, after obtaining from Hodges the latest
reports from the front, were to shorten the American line and to
begin collecting an American reserve corps to be commanded by
General "Lightning Joe" Collins, who had led the great Cobra
breakout on July 25 in Normandy.

A wave of relief went through the staff of 1st U.S. Army. Neither
General Hodges nor General Simpson had seen General Bradley, their
12 U.S. Army Group commander, more than a couple of times in
recent weeks—and not once since the Germans launched their offensive on December 16. Now, here in person, was a fresh commander in chief whom Hodges knew from the Battle of Normandy—
a consummate professional who relished field command and had
experience of taking over a defeated army, as he had done in Egypt in
the summer of 1942. A man intent upon imposing his will, both on
his own commanders and on those of the enemy.

Under Montgomery's direct command 1st and 9th U.S. Armies
would now be responsible for the line from the Roermond area to
the southern flank of the German salient, at La Roche. Beyond La
Roche, the hastily summoned elements of 10th U.S. Armored Division and 101 U.S. Airborne division at Bastogne would pass to Patton's
3rd U.S. Army, whose forces were currently making their way north
from the Luxembourg area.

In fact, as Patton's biographer Carlo D'Este has pointed out,
Patton's three-division counterattack did not relieve Bastogne for
another six days—indeed Patton favored evacuating Bastogne until
it was explained to him how important the city was to the Germans
as a road hub. Moreover Patton soon found the Germans counterattacking his flank as, on December 22, he began to move his III Corps
north. There were serious American tank losses, and some units were
forced to withdraw in places. Patton later accepted responsibility for
the delay. "It is probably my fault," he said, "because I had been
insisting on day and night attacks." He privately admitted that "it is
very difficult for armored units to operate at night" in such bad

weather and that his men became "too tired." What made the slow-ness galling, as D'Este writes, was the fact that "the relief of the Bastogne was made in a sector occupied by inferior German forma-tions," which nevertheless managed to hold up the relief of the city until December 26—ten days after the German offensive had begun.[5]

Instead of having his divisions attack on a narrow front, Patton had ordered them to advance across a front of almost thirty miles, through country perfect for defense. "His attacking forces wore them-selves down against [the German] Seventh Army's tough and elusive defenses," wrote the historian Peter Elstob.[6] Patton had, in fact, "com-mitted his forces too soon"[7]—and though the Bastogne garrison was saved, the attack had no effect on the advance of the main two Ger-man panzer armies to the north.

In truth, the real Battle of the Bulge was won in the bulge itself, north of Bastogne, D'Este conceded—especially at St. Vith, where valiant units of the U.S. 7th Armored Division held out against over-whelming odds for eight days, as the two main panzer armies—the Sixth and Seventh Panzer Armies under Generals Sepp Dietrich and Hasso von Manteuffel—stormed through the Ardennes and Mont-gomery reorganized the American front to thwart them.

Patton's major contribution to the Battle of the Bulge was there-fore not so much tactical as moral. He personally briefed the com-manders of seven of his U.S. divisions and, as D'Este wrote, "made it a point to be seen" traveling on the icy highways in "an open ar-mored jeep. . . . Daily he prowled the roads of the [Southern] Ardennes, sitting ramrod stiff, often with his arms folded, his face unsmiling. More than once his face froze. Word of his presence man-aged to filter through the amazing GI grapevine with astonishing rapidity, as did his words of praise for his troops, which were always, without fail, reported through the chain of command: 'The Old Man says . . .' or 'Georgie says. . . . '"[8]

Montgomery's take-over of command on December 20, 1944, was a similar moral turning point in the battle. He immediately re-stored confidence at 1st U.S. Army Headquarters (where for several days Lieutenant-General Hodges had been unable to give orders, having suffered a nervous collapse), visited all the forward battle commanders, assessed the strength of the American defenses and, as the battle entered its most vicious phase, ordered the survivors of St. Vith to withdraw rather than be captured. "They can come back with all honor. They come back to more secure positions," he ordered, having been to see for himself the situation. "They put up a wonderful show."[9]

As D'Este recorded, with the "exception of Patton, Montgomery was the only senior commander regularly to visit his troops at the Ardennes front."[10] Eisenhower kept himself under lock and key "like a POW" in his headquarters at Versailles and had a security officer impersonate him each day, and Bradley stayed in his Luxembourg hotel, both of them afraid of German assassination squads. Neither Eisenhower nor Bradley, the most senior American field commanders in Europe, were seen by their own troops during the Battle of the Bulge—and their communications with their subordinate field commanders was scandalously poor. "Very little news, gap still open. It is most disturbing that Supreme HQ should be without information later than about 36–48 hours," the Allied naval commander in chief, Admiral Ramsay, noted on a visit to Versailles on December 22. "It is only too clear that there is no Supreme Operational Command in existence. No master mind and therefore no staff of one."[11]

By contrast Montgomery's system of liaison officers, authorized now to visit every American formation under his command, gave him a unique picture not only of the actual battlefront line positions, but also of the morale and strength of individual units and formations. SHAEF had assured him that Patton's armored attack on December 23 would slice through the infantry of the German Seventh Army and into the flank of the Fifth Panzer Army, but as the days went by, it became clear that Patton's tankers would have difficulty simply reaching the beleaguered defenders of Bastogne, let alone penetrating further. "I shall have to deal unaided with both 5 and 6 Panzer Armies," Monty signaled to Brooke on 22 December.[12]

Montgomery did, indeed, deal with the German salient—bringing in 30 British Corps from Dempsey's 2nd British Army to hold the western extremity of the offensive, while assembling Collins' new U.S. Corps to strike into the increasingly extended northern flank of the German salient. It was, Monty felt, all very familiar—a rerun of the Battle of Alam Halfa.

Like the Battle of Alam Halfa, the Battle of the Bulge fell into two parts: blunting the German attack, and forcing the Germans to an ignominious retreat, pummeled from ground and air.

While American commanders and troops in the Bulge had cause to thank Montgomery for taking command of a deteriorating battle and for bringing order out of chaos, General Bradley felt understandably humiliated and blamed Eisenhower for having, once again, "caved in" to British pressure for a change in command. Neither then nor later would either Bradley or Eisenhower acknowledge that the Battle of the Bulge had been their own fault: that the nearly one hundred thousand American casualties suffered in the Ardennes were the result of Eisenhower's "broad-front/fight all along the line" policy and Bradley's obstinate refusal to keep the sides "balanced" by maintaining sufficient reserves in the region to meet a possible German counterattack. Their failure to exercise hands-on command and maintain first-class communications, and their "disappearance" from the battle for fear of assassination squads, merely added insult to American injury.

Thus while Montgomery visited his commanders and men in the field with his British pennant flying and his outriders and five stars mounted on the fender of his Rolls Royce, Bradley hid his new armored Cadillac in a garage and allowed his four-star insignia to be stripped off his jeep; indeed he kept entirely to his headquarters, situated in a Luxembourg hotel. There, with no first-hand knowledge of the front or of conditions in the Ardennes, he waited each day for news of Patton's counterattack—and began to imagine that, if Hodges could mount a similar counterattack in the north, he might create a repeat of Mortain, halting the German attack and entrapping the attackers, as he had done at Falaise.

Such a fantasy, without Allied air support and in the most terrible winter conditions known for years in the Ardennes, did not accord with Montgomery's view of the situation or his tactical strategy. The Germans were attacking in overwhelming strength, with three armies on a concentrated front, as in 1940. This did not alarm him since war, he knew, also favors the defender who is in position, rather than the attacker who must expose himself. Given the widespread misunderstanding of this important battle, it is important to emphasize that, from the beginning to the end, Montgomery saw the Battle of the Ardennes as a defensive battle, not an offensive one. Why, Monty reasoned, would anyone want him to mount an Allied offensive in the Ardennes, with no strategic goal to be won in the region? Why waste men's lives, unless there was an overwhelming victory to be gained there?

Having approved of Eisenhower's latest plan (drawn up in November), which called for mounting a pincer attack on the Ruhr from Holland and from the Saar—that is, to the north and to the south of the Ardennes—Montgomery saw no good reason to expend one more American or British life in the Ardennes than was strictly necessary. The Germans must be forced to admit the failure of Wacht am Rhein and withdraw for *fear* of their salient being cut off at the neck; he did not think the Allies really had the ground strength to cut off the salient. Nor did he feel it right to expend lives in attempting to attack the Germans at the neck of their salient, where they were strongest, since this would merely give the German defenders an opportunity to inflict unnecessary casualties on the Allies. The defensive Battle of Alam Halfa in August 1942 had removed the last Axis threat to Egypt, and had allowed the British to assemble their forces and prepare their own decisive offensive battle at Alamein. In December 1944, Monty saw the Battle of the Bulge as similar to the Battle of Alam Halfa, that is, as a defensive battle that, for a minimum of further Allied casualties, would blunt the German penetration, force the Germans to retreat after suffering irreplaceable losses, and end any further threat to Holland, Belgium, or France; it would then permit the Allies to mount their own offensives on ground of their own choosing, in their own time, with massive air support.

With absolute determination, therefore, Montgomery brought his British 30 Corps east of the Meuse to meet and block the tip of the German salient (which came within six miles of the river). Then, having lured the Germans beyond resupply, he ordered Collins to "jab" at the northern German flank, but not to incur heavy casualties. If Patton did the same on the southern flank, the Germans would, he knew, suffer debilitating casualties—especially once the weather improved and the Allied air forces were able to operate. Thus, the Allies would retain always the initiative, keeping their real strength for the next battle: the crossing of the Rhine, north of the Ardennes, the envelopment of the Ruhr, and the race to Berlin.

By rights, then, the Battle of the Bulge, followed by the Battle of Germany, should have been the crowning military achievement of Montgomery's professional career—the equivalent of Alam Halfa and Alamein, but writ large: involving four Allied armies and huge air forces, it would be a critical defensive battle leading to the great and decisive offensive battle that would end the war.

But it was not to be, in terms of Allied dissension and later historiography—for reasons that must fascinate every serious student of war and biography.

The Battle of the Bulge would be the fourth and last time Montgomery and Patton would fight in the same battle. In Tunisia, Patton had attacked at Gafsa and helped Montgomery's 8th Army to burst through the Gabes Gap. In Sicily, despite its botched ending, the two generals, as army commanders, had conquered the great Mediterranean island in thirty-eight days. In Normandy, Patton had exploited Montgomery's breakout from the Cherbourg peninsula to race around the German armies tied down in Normandy and stun both the Germans and the world. And in the Ardennes, both having been called in from outside the sector, the two generals had displayed their legendary qualities in snatching deliverance from the jaws of Allied defeat. But the partnership ended there—thanks to Montgomery's behavior towards Patton's boss, General Bradley.

Summoning Bradley to a meeting at his forward headquarters on Christmas Day, 1944, Monty deliberately humbled his American counterpart. The Allies had suffered a "bloody nose," as Monty phrased it, but they had, he went on, learned a lesson. For himself, Monty felt satisfied that he had saved two American armies in their hour of need, and as the new army group commander of the north, with two American armies under command as well as his British and Canadian armies, he would be in the best possible position to embark on his own Wacht am Rhein, that is, the Allied crossing of the Rhine and the Battle of Germany.

Bradley was mortified—determined that, even though Patton's forces still had not relieved Bastogne, the battle should be transformed from defensive to offensive. And Eisenhower, to Monty's chagrin, agreed. When Eisenhower finally ventured out from his virtual self-imprisonment in the Trianon Palace Hotel at Versailles on December 27, 1944—for the first time in eight days—to meet Montgomery at Hasselt Station in Belgium, the two men therefore disagreed, Montgomery objecting fiercely to the notion of incurring significant further casualties in the Ardennes, since it was not there that Monty wished to mount his next battle.

Montgomery felt that, having been locked up in the Trianon Palace Hotel throughout the battle, Eisenhower simply had no idea of the conditions in which American troops were fighting. The terrible losses that Patton's 3rd U.S. Army was incurring only proved his point, he felt—and he was right. By the end of January 1945, Patton's 3rd U.S. Army alone saw more than fifty thousand men killed, wounded, or missing in the Ardennes—just to relieve Bastogne and recapture Houffalize, the centerpoint of the initial German offensive, where his forces met up with Montgomery's, driving from the north, on January 16, 1945. After Houffalize, however, Montgomery saw no reason for the Allies to go much further. The Germans had failed in their supposed masterstroke: they had not reached the Meuse, let alone the North Sea and Antwerp; they had been forced to retreat, having suffered more than eighty thousand casualties in the extremely difficult terrain and having lost immense amounts of irreplaceable equipment. It was time for the Allies to use their regained initiative and strike elsewhere.

Like Eisenhower, General Bradley felt otherwise. He thought it was incumbent on the U.S. army to avenge its defeat by staging an offensive victory in the Ardennes and that, by refusing to mount an all-out counterstroke on the northern flank, Montgomery had missed a golden opportunity. On January 16, 1945—having been given back command of Hodges's 1st U.S. Army, but not of Simpson's 9th U.S. Army, which Montgomery would employ in his crossing of the Rhine—Bradley therefore dictated a special memorandum for the record, in which he complained that Eisenhower's decisions were favoring the British commanders over the American commanders. "In view of the fact that we have 61 American divisions committed to this theater as compared to a total of 16 British and Dominion troops, including one Polish division, I see no reason why it should be necessary to accede so much to British demands" Bradley declared—and added that "our interests should come first."

Had General Bradley performed better as commander of 12 U.S. Army Group after Normandy, of course, the justice of his complaint would have been more obvious, especially after the failure at Arnhem, the "Bridge Too Far." But Bradley had not performed well, as a strategist, a tactician, or a battlefront commander, and the ease with which Hitler's counteroffensive slammed through the middle of his American line in the Ardennes was a terrible indictment of his generalship. But Montgomery's personal humiliation of his colleague was unforgivable. Thereafter everything Bradley did seemed calculated, overtly and psychologically, to "get even" with Montgomery and the "Brits," as he referred to them, rather than with the Germans.

This was a tragedy. As the days went by Montgomery could see the schism opening up, but, lacking Eisenhower's skills at conciliation and compromise, he completely failed to prevent it. Vainly he held a press conference to appeal for Allied unity and support for General Eisenhower, on January 6, 1945, but it proved a disaster—pouring yet more fuel onto the troubled Anglo-American fire, and prompting General Bradley to hold his own press conference in Luxembourg.

Behind a semblance of politeness, war now raged between the Allies themselves. Since Patton had moved his Lucky Forward headquarters next to Bradley's in Luxembourg on December 19, 1944, he had continued to encourage Bradley in his hopes for a great offensive victory in the Ardennes. None eventuated. As Monty wrote to one of his former chiefs of staff in the War Office, Eisenhower continued to authorize the American fighting in the Ardennes for the sole purpose of "keeping Bradley employed offensively" there[13]— at the cost of yet more American casualties, but without any strategic purpose. Nor was it effective. Far from bringing German divisions to battle and "writing them off," as Bradley claimed he was doing by continuing the attack in the Ardennes, his intelligence staff reported that divisions of the German Sixth Panzer Army were withdrawing to the Eastern Front. By January 30, 1945, even Eisenhower's secretary was confiding in the supreme commander's desk diary, "We are not hurting the German very much. Although we are attacking in the Ardennes the German is moving troops away."[14]

To Monty, this was a sad finale to what should have been a model defensive battle before the real battle of Germany at last began.

We have not space here to follow Montgomery's final campaign in northwestern Europe. With an American army, a British army, and a Canadian army under his command Montgomery crossed the Rhine in overwhelming force on March 23, 1945. Five days later his 9th U.S. Army was racing towards the Elbe, with Dempsey's 2nd British Army on his left—with plans to race for Berlin.

It was at that point that Eisenhower cashed in his last chips. The Allies would not go to Berlin, he decreed. The 9th U.S. Army was ordered to leave Montgomery's command—and was subsequently halted before reaching the Elbe under Bradley's command. As supreme commander he had been in touch with Stalin, Eisenhower explained to Montgomery. Bradley's task, Eisenhower declared, would be to "mop up" the Ruhr, then turn south, leaving Berlin to the Soviets—even though it was deemed likely that most Germans in the capital would prefer to surrender to the western Allies rather than be overrun by the Russians.

The decision seemed—and was—incredible because Eisenhower hadn't consulted the Combined Chiefs of Staff or Roosevelt or Churchill. The blow hit Montgomery like a bullet—a "counterattack" not by the enemy but by the supreme commander, as Monty wrote to a colleague in the War Office—"All very dirty work, I fear."[15] Even Patton, racing into southern Germany with his 3rd U.S. Army two weeks later, was aghast. "Ike, I don't see how you figure that one. We had better take Berlin and quick," he told Eisenhower on April 13, 1945, as, with the Ruhr laboriously secured, Simpson's 9th U.S. Army gained a thirty-mile bridgehead over the Elbe, at Barby, with seven divisions, plenty of supplies, and only sixty more miles to Berlin. "[W]e could have ploughed across there within twenty-four hour hours and been in Berlin in twenty-four to forty-eight hours," Simpson later claimed—maintaining that they could even have taken Hitler alive.[16]

Bradley again disagreed, however; indeed, he predicted up to 400,000 casualties if the Allies elected to assault Berlin from the west. Eisenhower believed him as well as his intelligence staff's prediction that Hitler would send his forces into the Bavarian Alps to make a last-ditch stand, the so-called Southern Redoubt. American forces were thus ordered to prepare for a major battle in the south of Germany, and Patton's forces were stopped short of Prague.

Montgomery, shorn of American ground formations, was beside himself with frustration but impotent to counteract it. Deprived of his last American troops (at Bradley's vengeful insistence), he did not even have sufficient forces to ensure passage across the Elbe to Lübeck in time to secure the Danish peninsula before the Russians overran Denmark, and was forced to beg for American paratroops—a final demonstration that the British, who had landed in parity on D-Day, had become a subsidiary partner in the western military alliance.

Taking pity, Eisenhower assigned Montgomery an American airborne corps, thus belatedly permitting 21 Army Group to cross the Elbe, and 11th British Armoured Division to race to the Baltic to stop—just—Russian forces from sneaking into the Danish peninsula. Meanwhile British and Canadian divisions seized Bremen and Hamburg—the latter almost obliterated by Air Marshal "Bomber" Harris's firestorm treatment from the air. It was now but a matter of days before the war in Europe would end. On May 2, Hitler having committed suicide in Berlin on April 30, emissaries from the new German Führer, Admiral Doenitz, arrived at Montgomery's tactical headquarters on Lüneburg Heath to sue for an armistice.

It was there, on May 4, 1945 (and filmed and recorded by the BBC), in a simple camouflaged tent on the windswept heath, around a plain wooden table, each general signing with a two-penny dipping pen, that Field-Marshal Montgomery demanded and took the official unconditional surrender of all German forces on land and sea and in the air in northwest Germany, Holland, and Denmark. It was victory on the field of battle—but tinged with disappointment at the way the Allied triumph in Normandy had been squandered.

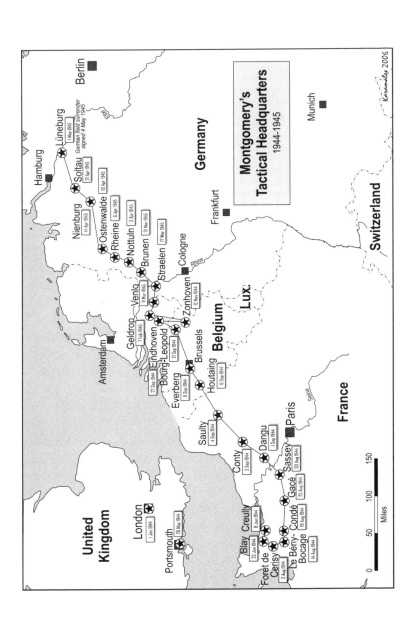

Montgomery's Tactical Headquarters

1944-1945

Germany

United Kingdom

France

Belgium

Lux.

Switzerland

Berlin

Munich

Hamburg

Lüneburg
1 May 1945
*German field surrender
signed 4 May 1945*

Soltau
25 Apr 1945

Nienburg
14 Apr 1945

Ostenwalde
8 Apr 1945

Rheine

Nottuln
3 Apr 1945

Brunen
30 Mar 1945

Straelen
17 Mar 1945

Venlo
8 Mar 1945

Geldrop
7 Feb 1945

Eindhoven
27 Sep 1944

Bourg-Leopold
23 Sep 1944

Everberg
8 Sep 1944

Houtaing
12 Sep 1944

Brussels

Zonhoven
12 Nov 1944

Cologne

Frankfurt

Rhine

Amsterdam

Saulty
4 Sep 1944

Conty
3 Sep 1944

Dangu
1 Sep 1944

Paris

Sassey
20 Aug 1944

Gacé
25 Aug 1944

Bény-
Condé
19 Aug 1944

Bocage
14 Aug 1944

Creully
8 Jun 1944

Blay
22 Jun 1944

Foret de
Cerisy
3 Aug 1944

Portsmouth

London
1 Jan 1944

Portsmouth
26 May 1944

Seine

Kosamitis 2006

0   50   100   150

Miles

Postwar

ONTY'S MILITARY career after World War II[1] became, ironically, almost as much a series of battles as the war had been. After serving as military governor of the British Zone of Occupation in Germany, as well as control commissioner for Berlin, he succeeded his revered boss, Field-Marshal Lord Alanbrooke, as chief of the imperial general staff (head of the British army). In that role, Montgomery was entrusted, under a Labour government, with the winding down of an empire that Britain could no longer afford to run. The task, which would have been difficult in itself, was made more so by the presence of Montgomery's old nemesis, Air Marshal Lord Tedder, in the position of head of the Royal Air Force. The two men were at such loggerheads they would not attend conferences of the three service chiefs together! It was clear that as a battlefield commander, Montgomery had been without peer. As a peer without an enemy he was a liability.

"Promoting" Montgomery to the first chairmanship of the Western Union's Commanders in Chief Committee, the Labour government then exiled Montgomery to France in 1949 to seek a new enemy: the Soviet Union. At Fontainebleau, attempting to lay the foundations of collective defense among the struggling postwar democracies of Europe, the field-marshal (he had been made a viscount, like Admiral Nelson, in 1946, but preferred his military title) soon found himself at similar loggerheads with his supposed subordinate, the European Land Forces commander in chief, General de Lattre de Tassigny—a nightmare that caused Montgomery finally to acknowledge that Dwight D. Eisenhower had been a great Allied general.

It was in this way that Montgomery came to press for and welcomed the return of American forces and an American supreme commander, charged with a new, anticommunist commitment to European defense. This was achieved through a new command organization in Europe, NATO, the North Atlantic Treaty Organization. Under General Eisenhower, who was appointed the first supreme commander Allied powers in Europe in 1951, and his American successors, Monty, already sixty-three, was made deputy supreme commander of NATO's forces in Europe and served in that capacity for almost a decade, until 1958—his main role being that of chief trainer and inspector general of NATO forces.

In the fall of 1958, celebrating fifty years as a British army officer, Montgomery retired and then stunned the world with the publication of his *Memoirs*—a narrative of his life and travails so candid and controversial that President Eisenhower and General Bradley, among others, virtually never spoke to him again!

Where Winston Churchill had shown magnanimity towards rivals and even opponents in his own account of World War II, Montgomery seemed determined to tell the truth as he saw it regardless of how many friends he lost in the process. Fame had gone to his head, and in the "evening of life" as he called it, the once anti-establishment "colonial" boy turned into an eccentric, conservative Englishman, a loose cannon whose views and rages no one could predict. He opposed a bill legitimizing homosexual relations between consenting adult males; supported apartheid in South Africa; visited Chairman Mao in China more than a decade before President Nixon's trip to Beijing; befriended Nikita Kruschev in the U.S.S.R., Marshal Tito of Yugoslavia, and Prime Minister Nehru of India; decried the American involvement in Vietnam as self-defeating; and deplored Britain's move to join the European Community and its common market. In the end the press grew weary of his antics. "Fade Away" (echoing MacArthur's famous words) was the plea one newspaper headline made to Montgomery, then in his eighties.

On March 24, 1976, at age 88, Montgomery finally did so. He had especially desired to outlive Churchill, his uneasy postwar friend and his greatest rival for public popularity in Britain. "Indomitable in retreat," Churchill had said of Monty, before his own death in 1965, "invincible in advance; insufferable in victory."[2]

Yet it was Monty's insufferable ego, as his famous chief of intelligence once remarked, that in World War II revived the military and civic morale of a struggling nation in its deadly confrontation with fascism. That same ego had become the dynamo of a desert army he made immortal in 1942. And it was that same ego, allied to an almost supernatural self-discipline and to an ability to make the once-defeated citizens of English democracy believe in themselves in a total war against the Third Reich, that made D-Day the most decisive and triumphant battle of the democracies in the twentieth century. For that alone Bernard Law Montgomery—"Monty"—will always be remembered. Not a "nice man," any more than Patton had been, as Monty's chief of intelligence was wont to remark, "but," the brigadier added, "nice men don't win wars."[3]

Notes

Preface
1. Drew Middleton, "Montgomery, Hard to Like or Ignore," *New York Times*, March 25, 1976.

Chapter 1
1. Nigel Hamilton, *Monty: The Making of a General, 1887–1942* (New York: McGraw Hill, 1981), 129.
2. Hamilton, *The Making of a General*, 160.
3. Hamilton, *The Making of a General*, 169.

Chapter 2
1. Nigel Hamilton, *The Full Monty: Montgomery of Alamein 1887–1942* (London: Allen Lane/Penguin, 2001), 363.
2. Winston Churchill, *History of the Second World War* (London: Cassell, 1951), 4:344.
3. Nigel Hamilton, *The Full Monty*, 593.
4. Paul Freyberg, *Bernard Freyberg VC: Soldier of Two Nations* (London: Hodder & Stoughton, 1991), 381.
5. Hamilton, *The Full Monty*, 477.
6. Hamilton, *The Full Monty*, 594.
7. Nigel Nicolson, ed., *Harold Nicolson, Diaries and Letters, 1939–1945* (London: Collins, 1967), 259.
8. Wendell Willkie, *One World* (New York: Simon & Schuster, 1943), 2.
9. Richard Overy, *Why the Allies Won* (London: Viking, 1995), 67.
10. Overy, *Why the Allies Won*, 283.

Chapter 3
1. Alun Chalfont, *Montgomery of Alamein* (London, 1976), 156.
2. Hamilton, *The Making of a General*, 623.
3. Ronalde Walker, *Alam Halfa and Alamein* (Wellington: Historical Publications Branch, Deparment of Internal Affairs, 1967), 180.

4. Willkie, *One World*, 7.
5. Hamilton, *The Making of a General*, 770.
6. Hamilton, *The Making of a General*, 763–64.
7. Gen. Sir Brian Horrocks, interview with author in Nigel Hamilton, *Monty: Master of the Battlefield, 1942–1944* (New York: McGraw Hill, 1984), caption opp. 161.
8. Hamilton, *The Making of a General*, 847.
9. Hamilton, *Master of the Battlefield*, 210–11.
10. Hamilton, *The Making of a General*, 175.
11. Hamilton, *Master of the Battlefield*, 213.
12. Omar Bradley with Clay Blair, *A General's Life* (New York: Simon & Schuster, 1983), 193.

Chapter 4
1. Bradley, *A General's Life*, 151.
2. Albert N. Garland and H. M. Smyth, *Sicily and the Surrender of Italy* (Washington, D.C.: U.S. Government Printing Office, 1965), 423.
3. See Hamilton, *The Making of a General*, 196–204.
4. Carlo D'Este, *Bitter Victory: The Battle for Sicily, 1943* (New York: E. P. Dutton, 1988), 545.
5. Carlo D'Este, *Eisenhower: A Soldier's Life* (New York: Henry Holt, 2002), 438.
6. Hamilton, *The Making of a General*, 348.
7. D'Este, *Bitter Victory*, 118.
8. D'Este, *Bitter Victory*, 553.

Chapter 5
1. D'Este, *Eisenhower*, 467.
2. Hamilton, *Master of the Battlefield*, 497.
3. Hamilton, *Master of the Battlefield*, 498.
4. Operation Jubilee was remounted on August 8, 1942, by Vice-Admiral Mountbatten, Chief of Combined Operations, largely for political reasons. See Hamilton, *The Full Monty*, 427–73, and Brian Villa, *Unauthorized Action: Mountbatten and the Dieppe Raid*, (Toronto: Oxford University Press, 1989).
5. Hamilton, *Master of the Battlefield*, 494.
6. Hamilton, *Master of the Battlefield*, 511–14.
7. Alfred D. Chandler, ed., *The Papers of Dwight David Eisenhower* (Baltimore: John Hopkins University Press, 1970), 3:1672.
8. An exceptionally clear account of the success of Fortitude is given in Stanley A. Hirshon, *General Patton: A Soldier's Life* (New York: HarperCollins, 2002), 471–96.

9. Hamilton, *Master of the Battlefield*, 559–64.
10. Hamilton, *Master of the Battlefield*, 515.
11. D'Este, *Eisenhower*, 470.
12. Chalfont, *Montgomery of Alamein*, 217.
13. Hamilton, *Master of the Battlefield*, 557.
14. John Ellis, *Brute Force: Allied Strategy and Tactics in the Second World War* (New York: Viking, 1990), 538–39.
15. Hamilton, *Master of the Battlefield*, 495.
16. D'Este, *Decision in Normandy* (New York: E. P. Dutton, 1983), 108.
17. Diary entry, June 5, 1944, in Arthur Bryant, *Triumph in the West*, (London: Collins, 1959), 205–6.
18. Hamilton, *Master of the Battlefield*, 591–92.
19. Alan Moorehead, *Montgomery* (London: Hamish Hamilton, 1946), 196.
20. Hamilton, *Master of the Battlefield*, 601.
21. Hamilton, *Master of the Battlefield*, 601.
22. Hamilton, *Master of the Battlefield*, 605.
23. Hamilton, *Master of the Battlefield*, 546.
24. D'Este, *Eisenhower*, 502.
25. Omar N. Bradley, *A Soldier's Story* (New York: Henry Holt, 1951), 209.

Chapter 6

1. D'Este, *Decision in Normandy*, 302.
2. Robert Graves, *Goodbye to All That* (Harmondsworth: Penguin, 1977), 107.
3. Bradley, *A General's Life*, 234.
4. D'Este, *Decision in Normandy*, 466.
5. D'Este, *Eisenhower*, 553.
6. Patton's refusal to credit the strategy behind Monty's patient tactical performance in Normandy was well reported by Basil Liddell Hart on June 19, 1944, after a visit to Patton—see Hirshon, *General Patton*, 481–82.
7. Martin Blumenson, ed., *The Patton Papers*, vol. 2, 1940–1945, (Boston: Houghton Mifflin, 1974), 479.
8. Hamilton, *Master of the Battlefield*, 723.
9. Hamilton, *Master of the Battlefield*, 728.
10. July 8, 1944, diary entry, in Hamilton, *Master of the Battlefield*, 731.
11. Hamilton, *Master of the Battlefield*, 737.
12. Hamilton, *Master of the Battlefield*, 739.
13. Chester B. Hansen diary, July 25, 1944, in Carlo D'Este, *Decision in Normandy*, 402.

14. Hamilton, *Master of the Battlefield*, 741.
15. Alanbrooke diary, entry of July 6, 1944, in Carlo D'Este, *Decision in Normandy*, 302.
16. D'Este, *Decision in Normandy*, 414–15.
17. D'Este, *Decision in Normandy*, 415.

Chapter 7
1. D'Este, *Decision in Normandy*, 72.
2. Hamilton, *Master of the Battlefield*, 798.
3. Hamilton, *Master of the Battlefield*, 798.
4. Hamilton, *Master of the Battlefield*, 807.
5. Hamilton, *Master of the Battlefield*, 791.
6. Hamilton, *The Field-Marshal*, 29.
7. Hamilton, *The Field-Marshal*, 22.
8. Hamilton, *The Field-Marshal*, 104–5.

Chapter 8
1. D'Este, *Eisenhower*, 643.
2. D'Este, *Patton*, 681.
3. Hamilton, *The Field-Marshal*, 193.
4. Hamilton, *The Field-Marshal*, 211.
5. D'Este, *Patton*, 699.
6. Peter Elstob, *Bastogne: The Road Block* (London: Macdonald), 1968, quoted in D'Este, *Patton*, 699.
7. D'Este, *Patton*, 699.
8. D'Este, *Patton*, 688.
9. H. M. Cole, *The Ardennes* (Washington, D.C.: U.S. Government Printing Office, 1965), 413.
10. D'Este, *Eisenhower*, 653.
11. Hamilton, *The Field-Marshal*, 231.
12. Hamilton, *The Field-Marshal*, 223.
13. Hamilton, *The Field-Marshal*, 339.
14. Hamilton, *The Field-Marshal*, 352.
15. Hamilton, *Master of the Battlefield*, 443.
16. Hamilton, *The Field-Marshal*, 479–80.

Chapter 9
1. See Hamilton, *The Field-Marshal, 1944–1976*.
2. Quoted in Carlo D'Este, *Eisenhower*, 407.
3. Nigel Hamilton, *Monty: The Man Behind the Legend* (Wheathampstead, England: Lennard Publishing, 1987), 114.

Bibliographic Note

Like most of the other senior commanders of World War II, Field-Marshal Montgomery retained or purloined most of his important military papers after the Allied victory in 1945. These were sold to the Thomson Organisation during his lifetime, and given to the Imperial War Museum (IWM), London, after his death in 1976. They have been augmented by gifts and deposits of further materials by Montgomery's son, the second Viscount Montgomery of Alamein; by Monty's chief of staff, Maj.-Gen. Sir Francis de Guingand; by Lt.-Col. Sir Denis Hamilton (whose newspaper serialized Montgomery's *Memoirs* and employed the field-marshal as a consultant writer); and by many of the field-marshal's colleagues and subordinates, including his chief of staff at the War Office, Lt.-Gen. Frank "Simbo" Simpson and his chief of intelligence in World War II, Brigadier Sir Edgar "Bill" Williams. Montgomery was a prolific letter-writer, and the IWM Montgomery collection—perhaps the largest deposit of records on a British wartime general—contains all Montgomery's diaries and extant World War I letters to his family, as well as the bulk of his letters to colleagues from the interwar period, World War II, and the postwar periods, either in original or in facsimile. The Department of Documents at the IWM also holds those records of this author that relate to his role as official biographer of Field-Marshal Montgomery, including audiotaped interviews with most of Montgomery's family, friends, and military colleagues who were alive in the ten years from 1977 to 1987.

Clearly, then, any researcher interested in primary documents regarding the life and career of Bernard Montgomery must begin by consulting the Department of Documents at the IWM, London. Other major archival holdings of Montgomery letters and materials—handwritten as well as typed originals, kept by the recipients, including Basil Liddell Hart, Sir Arthur Bryant, and Field-Marshal Lord Alanbrooke—as well as Monty-related documents donated by officers and historians who knew Montgomery, are to be found at the Liddell Hart Centre for Military Archives, King's College, London; the National Archives (Public Record Office), Kew; Churchill College Archives, Cambridge; the Bodleian, Oxford; the National Army Museum, London; Southampton University; the (U.S.) National Archives II, College Park, Maryland; the Eisenhower Presidential Library, Abilene, Texas; and the U.S. Army Military History Institute, Carlisle Barracks, Pennsylvania.

In addition the literature about the life and career of Field-Marshal Montgomery is extensive and continues to increase, each generation of historians adding and subtracting perspectives on this most controversial World War II commander.

Montgomery historiography has taken a somewhat cyclical course since 1945. At the conclusion of World War II Montgomery found himself an international hero, as popular as Horatio Nelson had been after 1805. Having survived his own Trafalgar, however, Montgomery was boastful enough to wish, like Churchill and, later, Alanbrooke, to "win the war twice: first in battle, then in print," as Brig. Sir Edgar Williams put it. Montgomery's own accounts of his supposedly error-free World War II campaigns were published soon after the end of hostilities as *El Alamein to the River Sangro* (Germany: Printing and Stationery Service, British Army of the Rhine, 1946) and *From Normandy to the Baltic* (London: Hutchinson, 1947), alongside Alan Moorehead's respectful biography (*Montgomery*, London: Cassell, 1946). Unfortunately, Montgomery's boastfulness, though it allowed him as an inveterate teacher to explain his military methods and skewer those who had crossed him, did not endear him to readers who resented his personal vanity and lack of magnanimity. Many of his enemies—some of them his own countrymen and wounded allies—were still alive. Irritated by Montgomery's constant self-praise, they became only too willing to give counter-versions, either in books, articles, and letters to the press, or in interviews with historians and journalists. Thus, from the start, works on Montgomery devolved into two camps, pro and contra, with few writers in the middle. For cultural reasons as much as for military-historiographical reasons, the contra camp has so far prevailed in the United States, while the pro camp has proved the more powerful in Britain.

In the United States, in the aftermath of World War II, there quickly arose three strands of anti-Montgomery literature: those works that reflected a conscious or unconscious resentment of the fact that a British general had commanded the U.S. armies in the great D-Day landings and the Battle of Normandy; those that took issue with Montgomery's strategic and tactical prosecution of World War II, especially in Sicily, Normandy, and northwestern Europe; and those who were outraged by his cocksure, egocentric, and dismissive personality. Beginning with Ralph Ingersoll's *Top Secret* (New York: Harcourt, Brace) in 1946 and Kay Summersby's *Eisenhower Was My Boss* (New York: Prentice Hall) in 1948, the postwar tide ran more and more strongly against Montgomery, especially after publication of his *Memoirs* in 1958, while General Eisenhower was still president of the United States. The film *Patton*, which won multiple Oscars in 1969, may be seen to have cemented the ever-growing prejudice against Montgomery in the United States, which has lasted to the present day. Stephen Ambrose, author of *The Supreme Commander* (New York: Doubleday, 1970) and *Eisenhower: Soldier, General of the Army, President-Elect, 1890–1952* (New York: Simon & Schuster, 1983), became the most popular and outspoken American excoriator of Montgomery; it was Ambrose who, as historical consultant to Stephen Spielberg's film *Saving Private Ryan*, was responsible for the single mention of Montgomery as Allied commander in chief of the D-Day armies: "a most overrated general." More serious American military historians such as official historian Gordon Harrison, in *Cross Channel Attack* (Washington, D.C.: Office of the Chief of Military History, 1951); Forrest Pogue, in *The Supreme Command* (Washington, D.C.: Office of the Chief of Military History, 1954); and Russell F. Weigley, in *Eisenhower's Lieutenants* (Bloomington: Indiana University Press, 1981), as well as Carlo D'Este in *Decision in Normandy*

(New York: Dutton, 1983), *Bitter Victory* (New York: Dutton, 1988), *Patton: A Genius For War* (New York: HarperCollins, 1995), and *Eisenhower: A Soldier's Life* (New York: Henry Holt, 2002), were at pains to give Montgomery credit at least for his professional wartime leadership, however obnoxious his personality. But their accounts have not prevailed against a largely negative popular view of Montgomery. In his justly Pulitzer Prize–winning account of the Allied campaign in North Africa, *An Army At Dawn* (New York: Henry Holt, 2002), Rick Atkinson acknowledged that Montgomery's men "trusted him to win," but also declares that, given that Montgomery was so "puerile, petty, and egocentric, bereft of irony, humility, and a sense of proportion," he could barely understand why.

In Britain, Montgomery's professional reputation underwent a similar postwar onslaught at the hands of historians and biographers such as R. W. Thompson, John Connell, Correlli Barnett, Alun Chalfont, Philip Warner, and F. H. Hinsley (see below), who all sought to downgrade Montgomery as a military commander, particularly on account of his lack of retrospective magnanimity towards colleagues such as General Lord Gort at Dunkirk and General Sir Claude Auckinleck at "First" Alamein. For a time, in the period between 1960 and the early 1980s, it looked as if British scholarship would demote Montgomery to the bottom ranks of the great modern field commanders, as American scholarship had done; indeed, if in the end Montgomery's reputation managed to survive such beatings in the U.K. and Commonwealth, it was perhaps only because, at the time, there were no credible alternative British generals with whom to contrast him, whereas American historians and readers had leaders such as Eisenhower, Patton, and Bradley. In the Mediterranean and European theaters of World War II operations, British historians were forced to concede that the performance of British senior commanders between 1939 and 1942 was abysmal. Generals like Gort, Ironside, Wavell, Auchinleck, Cunningham, and Ritchie simply failed to match their German opponents in battle, whereas for all his boastfulness, Montgomery did, triumphantly, at Alamein and thereafter. However much caustic writers cast around for alternative, more attractive heroes, the British cupboard was bare. General (later Field-

Marshal) Sir Harold Alexander, for example, fulfilled Churchill's ideal of a World War II general: son of an earl, debonair-looking, brave, charming, a fellow Harrovian, and blessed with beautiful manners. However, only two writers, Nigel Nicolson (who had served under Alexander as a Guards infantry officer) and David Hunt (who had served as Alexander's chief of intelligence), ever came forward to laud Alexander as a military hero; all other historians were either indifferent or openly contemptuous.

Thus, for all his lack of the gentlemanly qualities of deference to superiors, politeness, and magnanimity, Montgomery kept his reputation as the most successful battlefield general produced by Britain in World War II, however flawed the conduct of his campaigns. With the publication of many of Montgomery's letters, diary entries, signals, and memoranda in this author's official three-volume biography in the 1980s—Nigel Hamilton, *Monty: The Making of a General, 1887–1942*; *Monty: Master of the Battlefield, 1942–1944*; *Monty: The Field-Marshal, 1944–1976* (London: Hamish Hamilton, 1981, 1984, and 1986)—British and Commonwealth readers were able at last to judge Montgomery and his rise to power as an army commander in the field in its proper context, including the trials and tribulations of conducting modern war against a highly professional army serving a totalitarian enemy such as Germany. This left serious British historians to question only Montgomery's tactical mistakes (such as the pursuit of Rommel in the immediate aftermath of Alamein in 1942, his slowness to race to the rescue of Mark Clark at Salerno in 1943, the failure of Operation Goodwood, his slowness in seizing airfields south of Caen, the failure to fully close the Falaise gap, and the misadventure at Arnhem in 1944, as well as the ponderous crossing of the Rhine in March 1945), while acknowledging his unique positive qualities as a modern professional field commander.

Montgomery was a lifetime student of the art of war; a gifted staff officer; a brilliant teacher; a superlative trainer of officers and men, especially volunteers and conscripts; an inspiring speaker with a profound understanding and grasp of army morale; a revolutionary in his insistence upon pre-battle planning and rehearsal; an arch proponent of simplicity, air support, and cooperation of all arms and services; a master of modern communications and mobile, front-line headquarters; a great user of Allied intelligence and the art of deception; a master tactician on the battlefield; and a commander with a will of iron in the midst of battle. Historians ultimately acknowledged that Montgomery's positive qualities collectively raised him head and shoulders above any British contemporary. Indeed, save for General Patton—who never commanded an army group—they raised him above any other American or European Allied battlefield contemporary. Montgomery had almost single-handedly rescued Britain's professional military prowess from its amateurism and defeat in the early years of World War II, and he obliterated the indifference to casualties and the rear-headquarter luxury characterized by the generals of World War I, creating a standard for professionalism, communications, training, inspiring leadership, and personnel management that endures in the British army to this day. It was an extraordinary achievement.

Aside from Montgomery's two World War II campaign histories (produced by his staff from his papers) and his controversial *Memoirs* (London: Collins, 1958) only one volume of Montgomery's edited papers has so far been published: Stephen Brooks's excellent *Montgomery and the Eighth Army* (London: Army Records Society, 1991). Books by British official historians have been remarkably even-handed with Montgomery, however, and include I. S. O. Playfair's *The Mediterranean and Middle East*, volumes 3 and 4 (London: HMSO, 1966), and L. F. Ellis's *The War in France and Flanders* (London: HMSO, 1953, 1962) and *Victory in the West*, volumes 1 and 2 (London: HMSO, 1968). The Canadian Official Historian C. P. Stacey's *The Victory Campaign* (Ottawa: Cloutier, 1960), Australian Official Historian Barton Maughan's *Tobruk and El Alamein* (Canberra: Australian War Memorial, 1966), and New Zealand Official Historian Ronald Walker's *Alam Halfa and Alamein* (Wellington: Historical Publications Branch, Department of Internal Affairs, 1967) tended to be more laudatory than their British counterparts—owing perhaps to the near-criminal casualties to soldiers of the British empire on the western front in World War I, and the tragic misuse of Commonwealth forces in World War II until Montgomery's arrival at Alamein.

A testament to Montgomery's unique leadership skills is the sheer number of positive works written by Montgomery's most talented subordinates in World War II. These include Francis de Guingand's *Operation Victory* (London: Hodder & Stoughton, 1947), *Generals At War* (London: Hodder & Stoughton, 1964), and *From Brass Hat to Bowler Hat* (London: Hamish Hamilton, 1979); Charles Richardson's *Flashback: A Soldier's Story* (London: Brassey's, 1985), David Belchem's *All in the Day's March* (London: Collins, 1978); Brian Horrocks's *A Full Life* (London: Collins, 1960) and *Corps Commander* (London: Collins 1977); Nigel Poett's *Pure Poett* (London: Leo Cooper, 1991); Goronwy Rees's *A Bundle of Sensations* (London: Chatto & Windus, 1960); G. P. B. "Pip" Roberts's *From the Desert to the Baltic* (London: Kimber, 1987); Francis Tuker's *Approach to Battle* (London: Cassell, 1963); Michael Carver's *Out of Step: Memoirs of a Field Marshal* (London: Hutchinson, 1989); and Carol Mather's *When the Grass Stops Growing: A War Memoir* (London: Leo Cooper, 1999).

British works analyzing and evaluating Montgomery's professional performance as a battlefield commander include E. K. G. Sixsmith's *British Generalship in the 20th Century* (London: Arms & Armour Press, 1970), Ronald Lewin's *Montgomery as Military Commander* (London: Batsford,1971), Michael Carver's *The Seven Ages of the British Army* (London: Weidenfeld & Nicolson, 1984), and Shelford Bidwell and Dominick Graham's *Fire-Power: British Army Weapons and Theories of War, 1904-1945* (London: Allen & Unwin, 1982).

Narrative accounts of Montgomery's military career include this author's official biography, published in three volumes: *Monty: The Making of a General, 1887–1942* (New York: McGraw Hill, 1981), *Master of the Battlefield, Monty's War Years, 1942–1944* (New York: McGraw Hill, 1984) and *Monty: Final Years of the Field Marshal, 1944–1976* (New York: McGraw Hill, 1986). The author's updated and revised account of Montgomery's life up to the end of the battle of Alamein, *The Full Monty: Montgomery of Alamein, 1887–1942*, followed in 2001 (London: Viking, Penguin). Adrian Stewart's *Eighth Army's Greatest Victories: Alam Halfa to Tunis, 1942–1943* (London: Pen and Sword, 1999) and Richard Lamb's *Montgomery in Europe, 1943-45* (London: Buchan & Enright, 1983) record and assess

Montgomery's role in two main theater campaigns as an army commander and as an army group commander, while Michael Carver's *El Alamein* (London: Batsford, 1962), C. E. Lucas Phillip's *Alamein* (London: Heinemann, 1973), James Lucas's *War in the Desert: The Eighth Army at Alamein* (London: Arms & Armour Press, 1982), Barrie Pitt's *The Crucible of War: Year of Alamein* (London: Cape, 1982), and John Strawson's *El Alamein: Desert Victory* (London: Dent, 1981) all address the battle which made Montgomery's name. A spate of sixtieth anniversary books have since appeared, including Jon Latimer's *Alamein* (London: John Murray, 2002), John Bierman and Colin Smith's *Alamein: War Without Hate* (London: Viking 2002), Stephen Bungay's *Alamein* (London: Aurum, 2003), and Tim Clayton and Phil Craig's *End of the Beginning* (London: Hodder & Stoughton, 2003). Books that provide critical justice to Montgomery's part in the Sicily, Italy, D-Day, and Normandy campaigns include Carlo D'Este's *Bitter Victory* (as above), Dominick Graham and Shelford Bidwell's *Tug of War: The Battle for Italy, 1943–1945* (London: Hodder & Stoughton, 1986), Max Hastings's *Overlord: D-Day and the Battle for Normandy, 1944* (New York: Simon & Schuster, 1984), Carlo D'Este's *Decision in Normandy* (as above), and John Keegan's *Six Armies in Normandy* (New York: Viking, 1982).

British military literature largely hostile to Montgomery, as mentioned above, is amply represented by John Connell's *Auchinleck* (London: Cassell, 1959), Correlli Barnett's *The Desert Generals* (London: Kimber, 1960), Lord Tedder's *With Prejudice* (London: Cassell, 1966), R. W. Thompson's *The Montgomery Legend* (London: Allen & Unwin, 1967), Alun Chalfont's *Montgomery of Alamein* (London: Weidenfeld & Nicolson, 1976), Roger Parkinson's *The Auk: Victor at Alamein* (London: Hart-Davis MacGibbon, 1977), Philip Warner's *Auchinleck: The Lonely Soldier* (London: Buchan & Enright, 1981) and John Ellis's *Brute Force* (London: Andre Deutsch 1990), as well as subsidiary squibs such as Robert Clarson-Leach's *Massacre at Alamein? Were Generals Wavell and Auchinleck Treated Unjustly and was Montgomery Over-rated During the Desert Wars of 1940–41, 1941–42 and 1942–43?* (Upton upon Severn: Square One, 1996).

The crucial role of Ultra in Montgomery's campaigns, meanwhile, is described in Ronald Lewin's *Ultra Goes to War* (London:

Hutchinson, 1978), Ralph Bennett's *Ultra and Mediterranean Strategy, 1941–1945* (London: Hamish Hamilton, 1989) and *Ultra in the West* (London: Hutchinson, 1979), as well as in F. H. Hinsley's somewhat pejorative *British Intelligence in the Second World War: Its Influence on Strategy and Operations*, volumes 2 and 3 (parts 1 and 2) (London: HMSO, 1981, 1984, and 1985), in which Hinsley maintains a spurious objectivity by giving no names apart from celebrities' names. The vital role of deception in Montgomery's battle planning is, however, more accurately featured in Charles Cruickshanks's *Deception in World War II* (Oxford: Oxford University Press, 1981).

Montgomery's difficult relationships with his peers also are a feature of postwar military history and biography. His relationship with Winston Churchill, for example, is recorded, inter alia, in Martin Gilbert's magisterial *The Road to Victory: Winston S. Churchill, 1941–1945* (London: Heinemann, 1986); his crucial relationship with Alanbrooke in Arthur Bryant's *The Turn of the Tide* (London: Collins, 1957) and *Triumph in the West* (London: Collins, 1959), David Fraser's *Alanbrooke* (London: Collins, 1982), as well as Alex Danchev and Daniel Todman's edition of Alanbrooke's papers, *War Diaries, 1941–1945: Field Marshal Lord Alanbrooke* (London: Weidenfeld & Nicolson, 2001). Montgomery's insubordination to his commander in the field, Gen. Harold Alexander, is well recounted in Nigel Nicolson's *Alex* (New York: Athenaeum, 1973) and David Hunt's *A Don At War* (London: Kimber, 1966); his relationship with the military historian and guru Basil Liddell-Hart in Alex Danchev's magical *The Alchemist of War* (London: Kimber, 1998); his relationship with Eisenhower in Carlo D'Este's *Eisenhower: A Soldier's Life* (as above); with Bradley in Omar Bradley's *A General's Life*, written by Clay Blair (New York: Simon & Schuster, 1983); and with Patton in Martin Blumenson's two-volume edition of *The Patton Papers* (Boston: Houghton Mifflin, 1972 and 1974) as well as Carlo D'Este's *Patton: A Genius For War* (as above) and Stanley P. Hirshon's *General Patton: A Soldier's Life* (New York: Harper Collins, 2002). Accounts of Rommel's battles against Montgomery and views on him are included in Desmond Young's *Rommel* (London: Collins, 1950), Basil Liddell Hart's edition of *The Rommel Papers* (New York: Harcourt Brace,

1953), David Irving's *The Trail of the Fox* (London: Weidenfeld & Nicolson, 1977), and David Fraser's *Knight's Cross: A Life of Field Marshal Erwin Rommel* (New York: Simon & Schuster, 1993).

Personal accounts by members of Montgomery's family include Brian Montgomery's *A Field Marshal in the Family* (London: Constable, 1973) and David Montgomery and Alistair Horne's *Monty: The Lonely Leader, 1944–1945* (New York: HarperCollins, 1994). Useful archival picture books include Victor Musgrave's *Montgomery: His Life in Pictures* (London: Sagall Press, 1947) and Brian Montgomery's *Monty: A Life in Photographs* (Poole, England: Blandford, 1985), as well as the author's illustrated *Monty: The Man Behind the Legend* (Wheathampstead, England: Lennard Publishing, 1987).

Further personal insight into Montgomery's character and *modus operandi* in war is contained in Anthony Brett-James's *Conversations with Montgomery* (London: Kimber, 1984) and David Howarth's *Monty at Close Quarters* (London: Leo Cooper, 1985), which features chapters by a number of Montgomery's closest associates and staff officers.

A BBC1 centenary documentary, *Monty: In Love and War*, directed by Jeremy Bennett, was produced in 1987, and included interviews with members of Montgomery's family and wartime staff, a number of whom are quoted in the author's accompanying book, *Monty: The Man Behind the Legend* (as above).

Finally, Colin F. Baxter wrote an excellent annotated, end-of-the-century detailed bibliography of the literature on Montgomery and his campaigns titled *Field Marshal Bernard Law Montgomery, 1887–1976: Selected Bibliography* (Westport, CT: Greenwood Press, 1999).

Meanwhile the literary war—now primarily a trans-Atlantic one—still continues.

About the Author

Nigel Hamilton is the author of the acclaimed three-volume official biography of the legendary World War II commander Field-Marshal Bernard Montgomery, *Monty*, which won the Whitbread Prize and the Templer Medal. He is also the author of *The Brothers Mann*, *JFK: Reckless Youth*, and *Bill Clinton: An American Journey*. Currently a visiting fellow in the John W. McCormack Graduate School of Policy Studies, University of Massachusetts, Boston, Hamilton lives in Somerville, Massachusetts.